HARCOURT SCHOOL PUBLISHERS

STORYtown

CATCH A WAVE

Harcourt

SCHOOL PUBLISHERS

www.harcourtschool.com

ISBN 0-15-354539-9
ISBN 978-0-15-354539-9

4 5 6 7 8 9 10 179 16 15 14 13 12 11 10 09 08

CONTENTS

coaxed
expectations
fringes
hesitating
humiliation
sincere

Vocabulary

Build Robust Vocabulary

Write the Vocabulary Word that completes each sentence in the letters. The first one has been done for you.

Dear Pat,

We aren't there yet. But the dogs are doing fine on the long trip. Dad said I'll like it there, but I'll miss you!

We stop a lot so the dogs can run. They do not have to be

(1) _____ coaxed _____ to get out.

I hope there are some fun kids on our block. And I hope they are like me and have dogs. I do not wish to be on the

(2) _____ with no pals. I have no

(3) _____ –just hope.

Your pal,
Kate

Dear Pat,

I like our block a lot! I made a pal—a kid named Dan. And he has a dog! What luck for me!

Dan's dog is named June. When Dan got June, she was acting up. She didn't do what Dan said, because he was **(4)** _____ as he spoke to her. I gave him some tips. I was risking **(5)** _____ . What if he said I was being rude? But for June's sake, I spoke up. I was glad I did.

Dan has a **(6)** _____ wish for his dog to be liked. I think he will do a fine job—with some tips from me!

I still miss you. I hope you can visit us in the spring. You'll like Dan and June!

Your pal,
Kate

NO Expectations

by Emily Hutchinson • illustrated by Aaron Jasinski

"Here you go, Dan," Dad said, handing me the rope. A dog was on it! "This dog is a fine dog. It's your job to care for her now. Can you do it?"

How difficult could it be? I took care of my fish just fine.

"I can do it, Dad," I said. I hadn't had a dog before. I had no expectations of how she'd act. **1**

Stop and Think

1 What do you think Dan will learn about caring for a dog?

I think Dan will learn that _____

_____

_____

The dog's name was June, but to me, she was Mad Dog. Mad Dog did just what she liked. And she liked banging into things, tipping over the trash can, and nipping at pants. I said, "June, sit," and she ran up and down, ripping up the grass. I said, "June, come," and she plopped down in the mud.

"Can you use a tip?" I looked over and there was Kate. She had just moved to our block. ❷

Stop and Think

❷ What problem does Dan have?

Dan's problem is _____

_____

_____

June jumped up on Kate. "June, do *not* jump," I said as I grabbed her. I was mad, but Kate was not. She had a sincere look as she spoke.

"You were hesitating when you spoke to her. That's not how I'd do it. Use a strong tone, look at her, and make her look at you."

In a strong tone, Kate said, "Sit," and June sat, *plop*, just like that. She didn't have to be coaxed at all. ❸

Stop and Think

❸ What tip does Kate tell Dan?

Kate tells Dan that _____

_____

_____

© Harcourt

14

Kate stroked June's back and said, "You cute thing, I have some carrots in my bag. Do you like carrots?"

Kate snapped off a bit of carrot, and June gulped it down. Kate patted her and said to me, "You can hand her a snack like a carrot as a thank-you.

"Dogs are a lot like you and me," Kate added. "They don't like to be on the fringes. They want to be liked, and they hate the humiliation when you're mad at them." **4**

Stop and Think

4 How do you think Kate feels about dogs?

I think Kate feels _____

_____

_____

"Now *you* do it," Kate insisted. She handed me a carrot stub.

"JUNE, SIT!" I yelled. Mad Dog stepped back so she wasn't so close to me.

"You don't have to scare her," Kate said.

I waved the carrot stub like a flag. "Sit!" This time she did it! ❺

Stop and Think

❺ How does Kate help Dan?

Kate helps Dan by _____

_____

_____

16

Then Kate got a stuffed duck out of her bag and wagged it in front of June's nose. She tossed it and said, "Get it, June!" June was off like a shot to get the duck; then she picked it up and dropped it back in Kate's hand. Down went a bit of carrot, *gulp, gulp*.

"This is fantastic, Kate," I said, "but how did you get to be a dog whiz? How did you get all these tips?"

"Come home with me and you will see," she said. **6**

Stop and Think

6 What do you think Dan will see?

I think he will see _____

_____

_____

At Kate's, six big dogs were running up and down on the grass out back, like fine-tuned athletes.

"I *do* see, Dog Whiz!" I said. "Thanks a lot for all the tips. Now what can *I* do for *you*?"

"I'm glad you asked," Kate said. "Get the tub and the hose over there. These dogs all need baths!"

So thanks to my dog, I now had a pal. And my Mad Dog? She had six of them! **7**

Stop and Think

7 Do you think Kate takes good care of her dogs? Explain.

I think that Kate _____

_____

_____

18

Think Critically

1. How is Dan's problem resolved? Copy the story map, and fill it in. PLOT

Characters		Setting

Plot Events

1. *Dan can't handle his dog, June.*

2.

3.

2. What did Dan learn about caring for a dog? CHARACTER

Dan learned that _____

_____

_____

_____

3. What did you learn about friendship and solving problems?
AUTHOR'S PURPOSE

I learned that _____

_____

_____

conceited

designated

exhilarated

maven

mortified

reigned

smirk

Vocabulary

Build Robust Vocabulary

Read the selection and think about the meanings of the words in dark type.

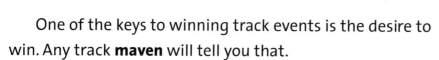

One of the keys to winning track events is the desire to win. Any track **maven** will tell you that.

Cathy Freeman had a big desire to win. And she did win! But sometimes she lost on the track. Some athletes are **mortified** when they don't win. Freeman didn't let her losses stop her. She just kept running.

Cathy Freeman led her track team to lots of big wins. She ran in the Olympic Games in 1996 and 2000. Then Freeman became the **designated** "Queen of the Track." She was **exhilarated** to be chosen as track queen. She **reigned** for years. But winning didn't make Freeman **conceited.** No one saw a **smirk** on her face. Freeman just kept on doing her best.

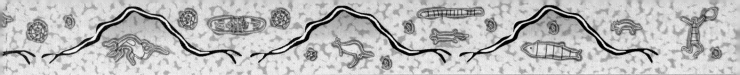

Write answers to these questions. Use complete
sentences. The first one has been done for you.

1. What is a track **maven**?

A track maven is someone who knows a lot

about winning track events.

2. What makes some athletes feel **mortified**?

_____

_____

3. How do you think Freeman became the **designated**

"Queen of the Track"?

_____

_____

4. How did Freeman feel when she **reigned** as "Queen of

the Track"?

_____

_____

5. What could make a **conceited** athlete **smirk**?

_____

_____

CATHY FREEMAN

by Emily Hutchinson • illustrated by Joe Lemonnier

As a kid in Queensland, Cathy Freeman could run quite fast. When Cathy was five, her teacher asked her to run in a contest. The teacher had a feeling that Cathy could win.

Cathy did win the contest. At the same time, she realized that she liked running. And she liked to win as well!

At six, she began to compete at track events. It was clear to Cathy what she wanted to do with her life. She *had* to run! ❶

CATHY FREEMAN IS FROM QUEENSLAND.

AUSTRALIA

QUEENSLAND

Stop and Think

❶ What do you know about Cathy Freeman so far?

I know that Cathy Freeman _____

_____

_____

Cathy spent all her free time running. Sometimes she ran laps in her bare feet on a grass track. And as she ran, she dreamed that she could be the best.

Cathy's stepfather liked to see her run. Noting Cathy's speed, he said that she could compete with the best athletes. He wished he could help make her dream happen. He asked a track coach to help Cathy run even faster. **2**

Stop and Think

2 Do you think Cathy's dream will come true? Explain.

I think Cathy's dream _____

_____

_____

At just sixteen, Cathy led her team to a big win in a contest in New Zealand. Her best speed just amazed those who got to see her run. People began to notice her at track events.

Cathy's coach at the time was a real track maven. He said that in all his years of coaching, he hadn't seen a talent like hers. Cathy Freeman's life on the track was off and running! ❸

Stop and Think

❸ Why was Freeman's life on the track "off and running"?

It was "off and running" because _____

_____

_____

Freeman's wins didn't make her conceited. No one saw a smirk on her face after a win. Her talent just made her see that her dream of winning big could happen.

Freeman didn't always win. Sometimes she lost on the track. Some people would be mortified if this happened. But Freeman didn't let the losses stop her. She felt deep down that she could still be the best. If she just kept at it, she could make it to the top. **4**

Stop and Think

4 What challenges did Freeman face? What did she do?

Freeman _____

_____

_____

CATHY FREEMAN IS "QUEEN OF THE TRACK."

In 1996, Freeman ran in the Olympic Games. The best athletes from across the land came to compete in these games. In one event, she finished in the fastest time of her life.

In the year 2000, Freeman was invited back to the Olympics. This time, she lit the flame to begin the games. She was exhilarated to be chosen for this respected task.

In those games, Cathy Freeman won the gold medal and became the designated "Queen of the Track." She reigned for years. **5**

Stop and Think

5 How do you think people felt about Freeman?

I think people felt _____

_____

_____

One time, Freeman was asked what the key to winning was. She replied that the key was to be in good shape. Just being in shape made her feel like she was the best, even when she didn't win.

Now, Freeman no longer competes in contests. She spends her time helping kids do their best. She helps kids deal with difficult feelings, such as sadness and fear. **6**

Stop and Think

6 Why does Freeman like to be in shape?

Freeman likes to be in shape because _____

_____

_____

While inspiring kids, Freeman teaches all of us a life lesson. "Life is what *you* make of it!" she once said. This attitude is what makes Freeman a winner. It's not her medals or her fame on the track. Freeman's desire to do her best makes her a winner on the track . . . and in life. **7**

Stop and Think

7 Think about Freeman's attitude. How can you be like Cathy Freeman?

I can be like Cathy Freeman by _____

_____

_____

© Harcourt

Think Critically

1. What do you learn about Cathy Freeman?

MAIN IDEA AND DETAILS

I learn that _____

_____

_____

2. How does Cathy Freeman reach her dream? Copy the story map, and fill it in. **PLOT**

Characters		Setting

Plot Events

1. *Cathy Freeman trains with a track coach.*
2.
3.
4.

3. Why does the author think that Cathy Freeman's story is important? AUTHOR'S PURPOSE

The author thinks that her story is important because

_____

_____

_____

Vocabulary

desperately

grudgingly

indignantly

pried

sneered

urgently

Build Robust Vocabulary

Write the Vocabulary Word that completes each sentence in the diary. The first one has been done for you.

March 13, 1953

The weekend is coming. My parents are going to sell

baseball gear at the mall. That's how they make money.

I make money from helping kids with their math.

I **(1)** _____ desperately _____ want a workshop.

I'll keep doing this job until I have the money for one.

I like to make models of small homes. Last week,

I was fixing one of them. The chimney broke as I

(2) _____ it from the top

of the model. A workshop could have helped. It will

take some time for me to save the money. I can

get by without a workshop for now. I don't

(3) _____ need one.

"Someday," I tell myself.

March 14, 1953

Today started out perfectly calm. All of a sudden, a strong wind hit. It swept down the street making a big mess! Then Dad called and said our stall had been hit by the wind. "Just one stall was crushed—ours," Mom said **(4)** _____ .

Mom and Dad can't make money without a stall. I went to get my savings. I wanted to help, not **(5)** _____ , but with gladness. Mom could have **(6)** _____ at the little bit I had, but she didn't. She was grateful.

I am going to go help clean up the stall now. I'll tell more when I get back.

Walt Helps Out

by Tom Gorman   illustrated by Ashley Mims

Walt peered out at the sidewalk, shocked at the mess. Trash cans had been tipped over, and branches had fallen from the trees. Earlier, gusts of wind had swept down the street. It had been the strongest wind Walt had seen since the big storm in the fall of 1950. **1**

Stop and Think

1 What caused the trash cans to fall over?

The trash cans fell over because _____

_____

_____

© Harcourt

Walt checked his watch. It was five fifteen, past time for Tim's math lesson. What could be keeping him?

Walt helped kids who needed a little help with math. Tim Hall was a smaller kid who came over each week. Walt liked his job. He was saving the cash he made for his secret project. He desperately wanted to fix up a workshop at home so he could make small models of homes. ❷

Stop and Think

❷ Why is Walt saving his money?

Walt is saving his money because _____

_____

_____

BRRRING! Someone was calling. His mom picked up the phone. *Was it Tim?* Walt wanted to ask.

"No!" Walt heard his mom say. "The stall is all we have! What will we do now?"

Walt was puzzled. His mom was talking about the stall that his parents rented to sell equipment for baseball games. **3**

Stop and Think

3 Why do you think Walt's mom is upset?

I think that she is upset because _____

_____

_____

"What is it, Mom?" Walt asked.

"Our stall was hit in all that wind," she said. "Dad said the back and top got crushed, and the baseballs, bats, and mitts are missing."

"Just one stall was crushed—ours," she added indignantly. "Without that stall, we won't be able to pay the rent." **4**

Stop and Think

4 What do you think will happen next?

I think that _____

_____

_____

Walt wanted to save for his workshop. But he couldn't stand to see his mom so upset. He reached for his wallet.

"Mom," he said, "you and Dad can take the cash I've saved. I want to help, not grudgingly, but with gladness."

"I don't want to take your savings, but it'll help us," his mom said. She could have sneered at Walt's small wad of cash, but she didn't. "Thank you, Walt. Now let's go see if we can fix the stall." **5**

Stop and Think

5 Why does Walt offer his money to his parents?

Walt offers his money because _____

_____

_____

Just then, Tim pedaled up on his bike and quickly jumped off the seat. "Stop!" he called urgently. Walt and his mom waited so Tim could catch up to them.

"I saw your stall," said Tim. "My dad and I got all your stuff into a safe spot."

"Thanks, Tim!" said Walt. "Will you come with us to help fix the stall?"

"You bet," said Tim. **6**

Stop and Think

6 Would you like to have a friend like Tim? Explain your answer.

I think that _____

_____

_____

At the stall, big branches sat on the crumpled walls. Walt's dad pried a branch from one side.

With just a quick look, Walt summed up how the stall was made.

"We can fix this!" he said. Walt called out his plans, and Tim jotted them down. In no time, a much stronger stall was standing.

"Walt," his mom said. "We couldn't have done this without you. Now, what about fixing up that workshop?" **7**

Stop and Think

7 What do you learn about using your talents?

I learn that _____

_____

_____

© Harcourt

Think Critically

1. What do you learn about Walt? Copy the chart, and fill it in. CHARACTER

Character's Traits	Character's Motives

2. What is the problem in the story? How is it solved? PLOT

The problem is _____

_____

It is solved when _____

_____

3. How does Walt's mom feel at the beginning of the story? How does she feel at the end? COMPARE AND CONTRAST

At the beginning, Walt's mom feels _____

_____

At the end, Walt's mom feels _____

_____

crusaded

disheartened

eccentric

faze

impassable

infuriated

relented

Vocabulary

Build Robust Vocabulary

Read the selection and think about the meanings of the words in dark type.

In Susan B. Anthony's time, women could not vote. Susan was **disheartened** by this. She **crusaded** long and hard. She hoped to get women the same freedoms as men.

A woman was expected to be at home. She was expected to have a husband and children. A woman who did not do this was seen as **eccentric.**

In 1872, it was time to vote for the next United States president. Susan went to cast her vote. A lot of men were **infuriated** by this. But this didn't **faze** Susan. She demanded to be let in. She tried to get past some men, but they were **impassable.** She kept asking to pass. At last, the men **relented** and let her in. Susan cast her vote, but she was arrested. What do you think happened after that?

Write answers to these questions. Use complete
sentences. The first one has been done for you.

1. What was Susan B. Anthony doing when she **crusaded**?
She was working to get women the same freedoms
_____

as men.
_____

2. What made Susan feel **disheartened**?

_____

_____

3. What made a woman seem **eccentric**?

_____

_____

4. Why were the men **infuriated**? How did Susan feel?

_____

_____

5. What did the men do? Describe what happened as the
impassable men **relented.**

_____

_____

When Susan B. Anthony VOTED

by Stephen Davis • illustrated by Joel Spector

When you hear the name Susan B. Anthony, what do you think? Some people think of a woman who crusaded long and hard to get the same freedoms men had. Some think of the fondness that started between Susan and Elizabeth Cady Stanton, and how these two got the freedom to vote for women.

Just who was Susan B. Anthony? ❶

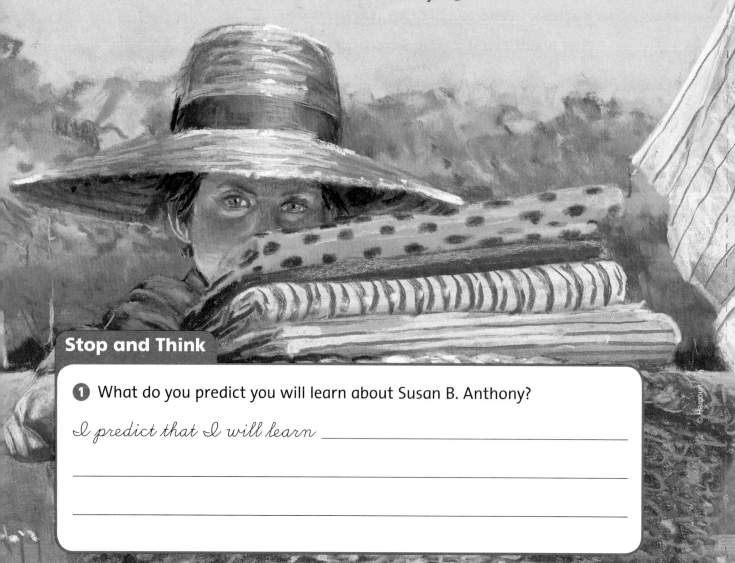

Stop and Think

❶ What do you predict you will learn about Susan B. Anthony?

I predict that I will learn _____

_____

_____

42

When Susan B. Anthony was little, a woman's life wasn't the same as it is now. A woman was expected to spend her time at home. She was expected to have a husband and children. She was to take care of the home and her garden. A woman wasn't pushed to be smart or take part in classes. The roles of a man and a woman seemed set and far apart. ❷

Stop and Think

❷ How was a woman's life in the 1800s different from a woman's life in the present?

In the 1800s, a woman _____

_____

_____

Susan's dad wanted his children to be treated the same. There was no separate treatment for his sons. Susan had the same lessons, the same tasks, and the same freedoms. Her dad wanted all of his children to be smart. He wanted each of them to make a mark in their lifetimes. ❸

Stop and Think

❸ Do you think Susan's dad believed men and women should have the same rights? Explain.

I think that Susan's dad _____

_____

_____

Susan B. Anthony did just that! She wanted to stand up for the freedom of all women.

Susan started to speak of her plans to people. Her speeches often sparked strong feelings among men. She was speaking of things they didn't like. Some didn't want women to have the same freedoms as men. Susan was seen as eccentric for those times. **4**

Stop and Think

4 How would you describe Susan B. Anthony?

Susan B. Anthony was _____

_____

_____

45

Then Susan met Elizabeth Cady Stanton. Elizabeth had the same strong feelings for freedom as Susan did.

At that time, a woman couldn't vote for a United States president. The two spoke to people of their desire to vote. Elizabeth wrote speeches, and Susan gave them. Susan spoke of a plan for a woman to be free to vote. Some men didn't agree. They wanted to keep Susan from speaking. But this didn't faze her. Susan just kept on crusading for women's freedom. **5**

Stop and Think

5 In what ways did Susan and Elizabeth make a good team?

Susan and Elizabeth made a good team because _____

_____

_____

In 1872, the next president was to be elected. Susan wanted to vote in this important election.

Susan went to the site to cast her vote. The volunteers who were taking up the ballots were quite startled when they saw her. They said she couldn't vote, but she demanded to be let in. The line of men was impassable, but Susan kept asking to pass. At last, the men relented and let her in. She filled out her card and cast her vote. No woman at that time had ever voted.

A lot of men were infuriated. They felt it was a crime for a woman to vote. Susan was arrested. **6**

Stop and Think

6 What happened after Susan voted?

After Susan voted, _____

_____

_____

Susan wasn't disheartened by her arrest. In fact, she felt it could help their plan. Elizabeth and Susan held marches and meetings across the land.

As the years passed, it was hard for Susan to go out and speak. So she asked others to keep her plan alive.

In 1920, the Nineteenth Amendment was passed. Finally, women were free to vote. Susan B. Anthony had made her mark in the end. **7**

Stop and Think

7 What problem did Susan face as she got older? How did she solve it?

As Susan got older, _____

_____

_____

Think Critically

1. What is the main idea of this selection? **MAIN IDEA**

    The main idea is _____

    _____

    _____

2. Why did Susan B. Anthony want women to vote? Copy the chart, and fill it in. **CHARACTER**

Character Traits	Character Motives
smart *fair and just* *strong*	

3. What does this story tell you about Susan B. Anthony? **AUTHOR'S PURPOSE**

    This story tells me that Susan B. Anthony _____

    _____

    _____

Vocabulary

Build Robust Vocabulary

Write the word that best completes each sentence.
The first one has been done for you.

1. The fifth-grade class is in a rush. They are

   _____**feverishly**_____ reading their lines

   grudgingly   indignantly   feverishly

   for this spring's play.

2. The stars _____ act out their

   indignantly   dramatically   eccentrically

   lines each day.

3. Despite being _____ with a small

   stricken   relented   genial

   case of the sniffles, one of the stars has not missed
   a day.

4. Addison said she didn't want to play the lead, but her

   _____ didn't work.

   prognostication   protest   maven

5. My _____ is that this will be the

   protest   smirk   prognostication

   best fifth-grade play ever. I can feel it!

6. Miss Garza leads the play each year. We like her big

smile and _____ ways.

genial   stricken   impassable

7. Miss Garza hopes this year's play is not a

_____ like last year's. It was a mess!

flop   protest   maven

8. All the kids want the play to be stunning and

_____ !

mortified   eccentric   spectacular

9. I can't _____ myself. We are fifth-

coax   restrain   faze

grade stars, the best yet!

10. I am _____ with excitement to be

conceited   spectacular   overcome

in this play!

Write the answers to these questions. Use complete sentences.

11. Why are the fifth-graders reading their lines feverishly?

_____

_____

12. What is a genial person like?

_____

_____

Twin Talent

by Carrie Waters

illustrated by Stacy Heller Budnock

STARRING . . .		
Narrator	**Addison**	**Ashton**
Miss Garza	**Devon**	**Gale**

Narrator: Ashton and Addison are twins who are always competing. In what way do they compete? You name it!

Ashton: Today's the day we read for parts in the class play, and I can't wait. I aim to be the next rising star!

Addison: No way, Ashton! I'm so afraid of public speaking that I can't even raise my hand in class.

Ashton: So I'll sail to stardom, and you'll be a flop. ❶

Stop and Think

❶ What do you learn about Addison and Ashton?

I learn that Addison and Ashton _____

_____

_____

Addison: You just can't restrain yourself, can you? You're glad I'm afraid! It's not like *you* haven't failed.

Gale: How did Ashton fail, Addison?

Addison: At the skating meet, I got a fantastic prize, but Ashton fell and had to be dragged across the rink on a sled.

Ashton: I sprained my ankle! I was in pain!

Devon: So this time, Addison fails, and Ashton wins.

Addison: Well, maybe they have a part for a standing lamp . . . **2**

Stop and Think

2 Why is Addison afraid?

Addison is afraid because _____

_____

_____

Narrator: Miss Garza, a genial teacher who always smiles, leads the class play. The readings are finished, and she is handing out the parts.

Miss Garza: Ashton, you will be stunning as our Tin Man.

Devon: Way to go!

Miss Garza: Addison, you've landed the leading role.

Gale: Hurray!

Narrator: Addison looks stricken with fear. **3**

Stop and Think

3 What do you think Addison will do?

I think Addison will _____

_____

_____

Addison: No way! I'm afraid of public speaking!

Miss Garza: Don't panic! I have faith in you.

Addison: But what if I'm overcome with fear and can't say a thing? What if I just plain forget my lines?

Miss Garza: I have a talent for prognostication, and I think you will be just fine.

Ashton: You have a talent for *what*?

Miss Garza: Prognostication—predicting what will happen. ❹

Stop and Think

❹ Why do you think Miss Garza wants Addison to be in the play?

I think she wants Addison to be in the play because _____

_____

_____

Narrator: Addison's protest didn't work. She is still playing the lead, and she and Ashton have spent days saying their lines over and over feverishly, to get them down pat. It's the day of the play.

Miss Garza: Greetings! Welcome to our class play!

Addison: I don't think this is Kansas, Toto!

Devon: Ashton is spectacular as the Tin Man . . . but he looks a little stiff. **5**

Stop and Think

5 Do you think Addison will perform well? Explain your answer.

I think that _____

_____

_____

Gale: Why isn't he saying something?

Narrator: Ashton is just standing there, like a big tin pail.

Addison: Umm, did you want to say something, Tin Man?

Narrator: It's plain that Ashton can't speak. This is terrible! Wait—Addison is saying something.

Addison: It *did* rain today, so maybe his tin lips are rusted shut. Just one second, please.

Devon: Why is Gale handing her a can? **6**

Stop and Think

6 How do you think Addison feels about Ashton now? How can you tell?

I think Addison feels _____

_____

_____

Narrator: Addison pretends to wipe grease on Ashton's lips. The play continues, with Ashton and Addison saying all of their lines.

Miss Garza: Ashton, despite the stiff start, you said all of your lines quite dramatically.

Ashton: But *you* saved the play, Addison. And you saved *me*! That's the end of competing for me!

Addison: You stick to that plan. Then, I can't miss winning the art contest.

Ashton: Wait, that's not fair! I'm fantastic at painting!

Gale: Here we go **7**

Stop and Think

7 How does Addison save the play?

Addison saves the play by _____

_____

_____

Think Critically

1. How do you think the story would have turned out differently if Ashton had been cast as the lead? **PLOT**

I think that _____

_____

_____

2. How are Addison and Ashton alike? How are they different? **COMPARE AND CONTRAST**

Here is how they are alike: _____

_____

Here is how they are different: _____

_____

3. What lesson do Addison and Ashton learn? **AUTHOR'S PURPOSE**

Addison and Ashton learn that _____

_____

_____

grateful

grim

irresistible

raspy

revelers

swarmed

wistful

Vocabulary

Build Robust Vocabulary

Write the Vocabulary Word that completes each sentence. The first one has been done for you.

Ray wanted a pal, but he didn't know anyone.

He felt **(1)** _____ wistful _____ . Down the

beach a bit, stalls were set up for a festival. A band was

playing to cheering **(2)** _____ .

Ray could see that they were having fun.

On the beach, seagulls **(3)** _____

as some kids fed them scraps. "I like this spot, Mom,"

Ray said. He was **(4)** _____ to

be there, but he wished he was having fun, too.

Ray's mom said he needed to go and meet some kids. Ray groaned.

"No need to look so **(5)** _____ ," his dad said. So Ray walked up the beach to look at the stalls.

One stall had handmade soaps and lemon drops to cure a **(6)** _____ throat. But Ray didn't like any of these things.

At last, Ray stumbled upon a stall that had kits for making model boats. There was one kit that was **(7)** _____ . Ray had to have it!

Write the answers to these questions. Use complete sentences.

8. What are revelers?

_____

_____

9. What does it mean to feel grateful?

_____

_____

Ray and Joan

by Cynthia Carroll

illustrated by Wayne Parmenter

Ray finished his poached eggs and toast, and looked out at the coastline. The sun sparkled on the water. Seagulls swarmed as some kids fed them scraps.

Ray watched a sailboat float along. Kids with kites ran on the sand. Down the beach a bit, stalls were set up for a festival, and a band was singing to the cheering revelers. **1**

Stop and Think

1 What can you tell about the setting?

I can tell that _____

_____

_____

"I like this spot, Mom," Ray said.

"I'm glad you like it," his mom said. "Now you need to get out there and meet some kids."

Ray groaned.

"No need to look so grim," his dad said. "You can just stay here and help me slap a coat of paint on the boat."

"I'm going! I'm going!" Ray walked up the beach to the festival to see the stalls. **2**

Stop and Think

2 How does Ray feel about making new friends?

Ray feels _____

_____

_____

One stall had plastic animals such as deer and toads to set out in gardens. One stall was selling pumpkin muffins and other breads. The next stall had handmade soaps and lemon drops to cure a raspy throat. But Ray didn't like any of these things.

At last, Ray stumbled upon a stall that he liked a lot. It held kits for making boat models. As Ray looked them over, the man in the stall spoke up.

"Do you like model boats?" he asked. **3**

Stop and Think

3 Which stall comes after the bread stall? Underline the sequence word.

After the bread stall, _____

_____

_____

Ray was a big fan of model boats. He had made model sailboats and steamboats. He had made boats of oak and pine. He had even carved boats out of bars of soap. He had made boats out of foam meat trays, plastic lids, and milk cartons. He was thinking of making a boat out of craft sticks next. It was safe to say that Ray was a fanatic when it came to model boats. So he nodded and said, "You bet! Do you?" **4**

Stop and Think

4 Why does the author describe all of Ray's boats?

The author describes Ray's boats because _____

_____

_____

"I used to make a lot of model boats when I was a kid," the man said. "Now I sell boat kits. My assistant makes the models. And here she is now!"

A kid with a nametag approached the stall. Ray could see that her name was Joan.

"Here you go, Dad," she said. "One roast beef sandwich on wheat bread."

"Joan made all the model boats," her dad boasted. **5**

Stop and Think

5 What do you learn about the man's assistant?

I learn that _____

_____

_____

© Harcourt

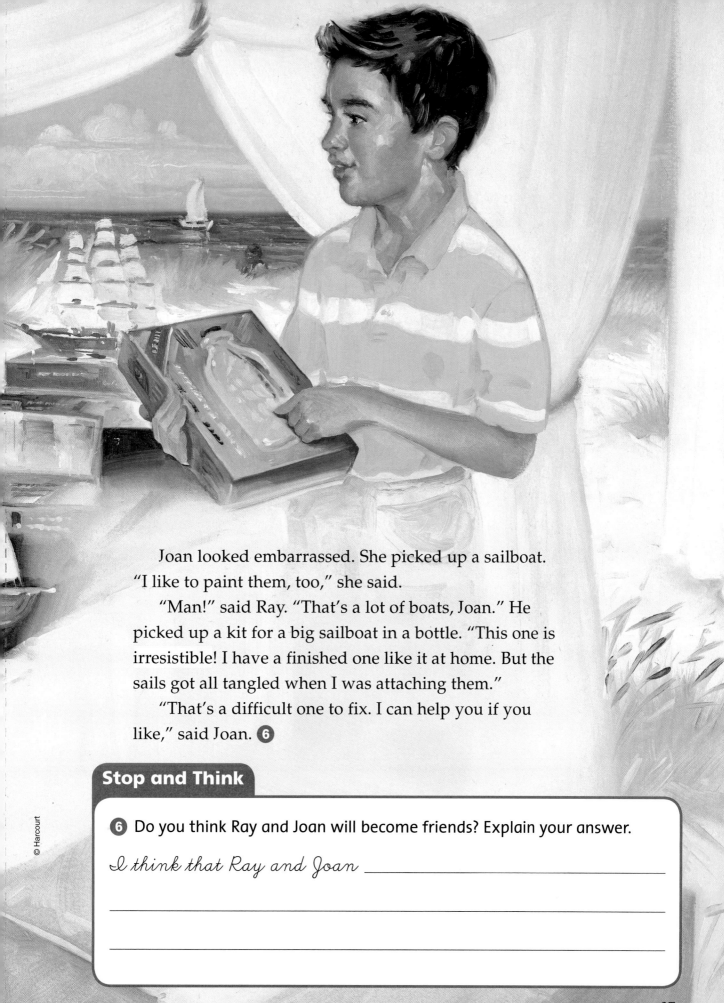

Joan looked embarrassed. She picked up a sailboat. "I like to paint them, too," she said.

"Man!" said Ray. "That's a lot of boats, Joan." He picked up a kit for a big sailboat in a bottle. "This one is irresistible! I have a finished one like it at home. But the sails got all tangled when I was attaching them."

"That's a difficult one to fix. I can help you if you like," said Joan. ⑥

Stop and Think

⑥ Do you think Ray and Joan will become friends? Explain your answer.

I think that Ray and Joan _____

_____

_____

"Thanks!" Ray was grateful for the help. "Just think," he said. "A long time back, real boats like this one used to sail in this bay."

Joan got a wistful look. "I've made all those model boats," she said. "But I haven't stepped on a real boat in my whole life."

"Now, that's simple to fix!" Ray grinned. "Come on. My mom will want to meet my boat-making pal. Just don't tell my dad that you like to paint boats!" ➐

Stop and Think

➐ How does Ray feel about making new friends now?

Now, Ray feels that _____

_____

_____

Think Critically

1. Think about Joan. How does she support the theme? Copy the chart, and fill it in. THEME

Character's Qualities	Character's Motives	Character's Actions
		offers to help Ray

Theme

It's easier to make friends when you share common interests.

2. How are Ray and Joan alike? How are they different? COMPARE AND CONTRAST

Here is how they are alike: _____

_____

Here is how they are different: _____

_____

_____

3. What happens after Ray meets Joan? PLOT

After Ray meets Joan, _____

_____

_____

| assured |

| fret |

| nudged |

| outlandish |

| proclaimed |

| ruckus |

Vocabulary

Build Robust Vocabulary

Write the Vocabulary Word that completes each sentence. The first one has been done for you.

"There will be a talent show," Mrs. Reed

(1) _____proclaimed_____ to the class.

Then, the day before the show, Owen got a big bump on his nose. "Now what?" he asked his pal Sara. "Tomorrow is the talent show!"

"Don't **(2)** _____ !" Sara said. She **(3)** _____ him that it would be okay.

Owen was not so sure. The growth on his nose was a big one. He didn't want to get up in front of all those kids.

Owen had an **(4)** _____ costume

for the talent show. It was very odd, but it helped to

hide his nose.

He met with Sara and Jack to go over their act.

They made such a **(5)** _____

that they scared away Jack's dog!

The next day, it was show time. Mrs. Reed

(6) _____ Owen. "Time to go on!"

she prodded him.

Owen was feeling a little tense. Will they like his

fake red nose?

Write the Vocabulary Word that best completes the synonym web.

7.

(be upset)   (be bothered)

(fuss)   _____   (dwell on something)

OWEN'S BIG SHOW

by Emily Hutchinson ★ illustrated by Karen Stormer Brooks

Owen had a problem—a big one. It was right in the middle of his nose! Some insect had bitten him, and the bite had grown into a big, red bump.

He called his pal Sara. "Now what?" he asked. "Tomorrow is the talent show. I can't get up in front of all those people. And I can't let you and Jack down after we've worked so hard on our act!" ❶

Stop and Think

❶ Why is Owen so upset about the bump on his nose?

Owen is upset because_____

_____

_____

72

"Slow down, Owen, and stay calm," said Sara. "Don't fret! What if you paint the lump red and make it part of the act?"

Sara's tip gave Owen the beginnings of a plan. He asked his mom to help him hollow out an old red ball and add a strip of elastic to it.

Stop and Think

2 How would you describe Sara?

I think Sara is _____

_____

_____

Then Owen dug his old scarecrow costume out of the closet. It was an outlandish get-up that included an over-sized fishing hat, a yellow wig, and a jacket with patched elbows. Owen topped it off with the hollow ball nose to hide his lump.

Soon, it was time to meet Sara and Jack at the willow tree to practice their act. **3**

Stop and Think

3 What do you know about Owen's costume? Underline the words that tell you this.

Owen's costume is _____

_____

_____

Owen arrived pushing a wheelbarrow full of props. Bud, Jack's dog, wanted to play with the balls when Owen started to juggle. Then Sara added her harmonica to the act, and the three pals made such a ruckus that Bud ran away to hide!

Then Jack came up with a better plan. "Why don't we *all* dress up like Owen?" he said.

"Yes!" agreed Owen and Sara. **4**

Stop and Think

4 Why do you think Jack suggests a new plan?

I think that Jack _____

_____

_____

The next day, at show time, Owen could see his mom and his Uncle Pete in their seats. Uncle Pete was the one who had shown Owen how to juggle. He hoped his uncle liked the show.

Just then, Mrs. Reed nudged Owen, who was feeling a little tense.

"Time to go on!" the teacher prodded.

"You'll do fine," Jack assured him. This was it. Owen and his pals started their act. **5**

Stop and Think

5 How do you think the show will go?

I think that _____

_____

_____

Owen began with balls that looked like bowling balls but were hollow. He juggled small beanbags, and then he juggled balls that glowed. The last thing he did was mix it all up, juggling small things and big things at the same time.

While Sara played her harmonica, Jack was blowing big bubbles to add to the fun. It was a swell act, and the three pals kept it all flowing. **6**

Stop and Think

6 What does Owen juggle first?

First, Owen juggles _____

_____

_____

© Harcourt

When they finished, all the kids rushed up, asking each of the stars to teach them their talents. Moms and dads rose up out of their seats, clapping. Owen's Uncle Pete proclaimed the show the best he had seen. Owen was so glad he had not let a little bump on his nose stop them from going on with the show. **7**

7 Do you think the friends should feel proud of their act? Explain.

I think the friends _____

_____

_____

© Harcourt

Think Critically

1. How did Owen solve his problem? **PLOT**

Owen solved his problem by _____

_____

_____

2. How did Sara and Jack help Owen? **CHARACTERS**

Sara and Jack helped Owen by _____

_____

_____

3. Think about Owen and his pals. What does this story teach
you about working together? Copy the chart, and fill it in.
AUTHOR'S PURPOSE

Character's Qualities	Character's Motives	Character's Actions
a good pal	wants to put on a good show	finds a way to hide his nose

Theme

appealed

crisis

crucial

destiny

encountered

maneuvered

perseverance

persuading

Vocabulary

Build Robust Vocabulary

Read the selection and think about the meanings of the words in dark type.

In 1773, colonists had to pay taxes to England. One tax was for tea. The colonists felt the tax was not fair. Some of them felt that their **destiny** was to be free from England. Leaders among the colonists **appealed** to the rest of them to stop drinking tea.

Three ships loaded with tea arrived in the port of Boston. The British said the ships had to stay until the colonists paid the tax on the tea. But the British **encountered** problems with the colonists. The colonists felt that **perseverance** was the key to getting what they wanted. **Persuading** the colonists to stay strong, Sam Adams said it was **crucial** that they not pay the tax.

The colonists made a plan to deal with the **crisis.** Between fifty and 250 men **maneuvered** their way onto the docks where the ships were moored. What do you think they did next?

© Harcourt

Write the answers to these questions. Use complete sentences. The first one has been done for you.

1. What did some colonists feel was their **destiny**?
   They felt their destiny was to be free from England.

2. What did leaders do when they **appealed** to the colonists?

   _____

   _____

3. What is a good way of **persuading** colonists not to drink tea?

   _____

4. What problems did the British **encounter**?

   _____

   _____

5. If **perseverance** is **crucial**, what must the colonists do?

   _____

   _____

6. What was the **crisis** in Boston?

   _____

7. Between fifty and 250 men **maneuvered** their way onto the docks. What do you think this means? Explain.

   _____

   _____

Tea Time in Boston

by Emily Hutchinson • illustrated by Dennis Lyall

It was 1773 in the port of Boston. There was a chill in the air. Colonists spent time indoors by the fire, sipping tea. Tea was an important part of life for them. They drank it all day, not just in the morning.

But tea drinking was becoming a problem. No one could grow tea in the colonies. They had to import tea from England. Then they had to pay an import tax. The money collected from the tax didn't go to Boston, but to England. **1**

Stop and Think

1 What problem did the colonists have?

The colonists _____

_____

_____

For a long time, England had taxed lots of things, such as salt and sugar. Now it was tea. According to the colonists, this wasn't fair, because they had no say in how the money was spent back in England.

Some colonists had sworn not to pay a single tax. They said their destiny was to be independent of England in all ways. They appealed to the rest of the colonists to stop drinking English tea. As a result, sales of tea went way down. **2**

Stop and Think

2 Why did sales of tea go down?

Sales of tea went down because _____

_____

_____

The prime minister of England, Lord North, ordered the tax to be reduced. Still, no one drank the tea. Perseverance, they felt, was the best way to get what they wanted.

In late 1773, shipments of tea were refused at some ports. At the port of Boston, three ships arrived. The order came from the governor to let the ships in. **3**

Stop and Think

3 Why do you think Lord North reduced the tax?

I think Lord North reduced the tax because _____

_____

_____

This made some of the colonists very angry. They didn't want the governor to accept this tea shipment because they didn't want to pay a tax on it.

Samuel Adams, a political leader in the colonies, held public meetings. Persuading the colonists to stay strong, he asked for their support. He said it was crucial that the ships leave without that tax being paid.

One ship started to leave, but the British stopped it. The British said the ship had to stay in the port until the tax on the tea was paid. **4**

Stop and Think

4 What do you think will happen next?

I think that _____

_____

_____

85

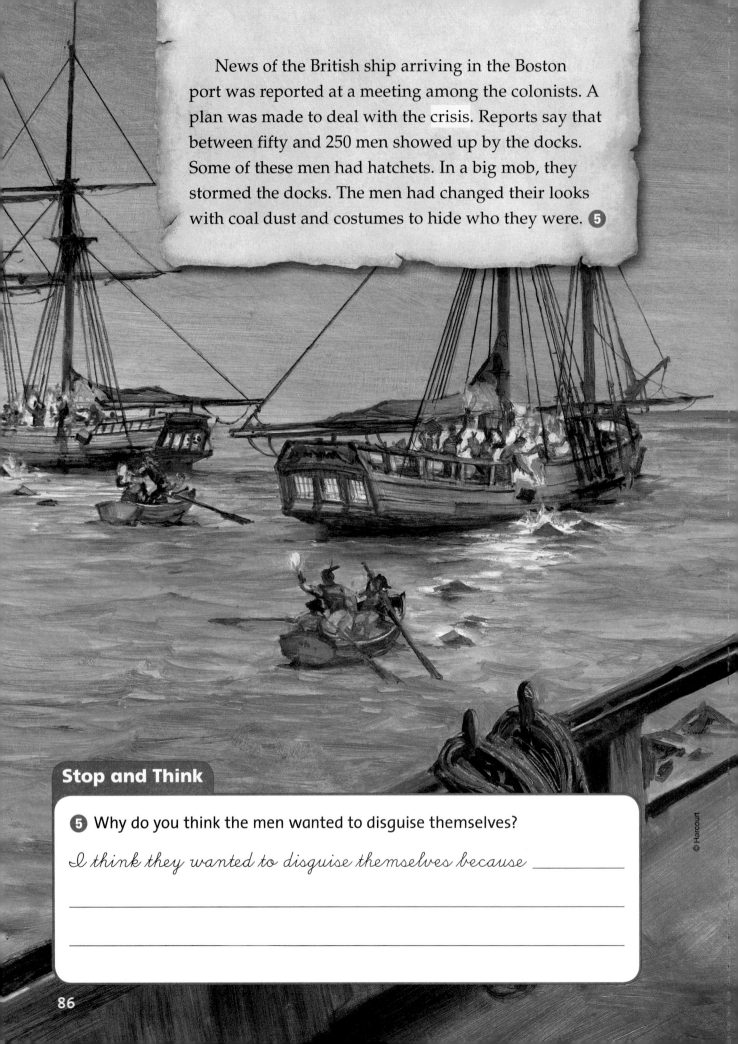

News of the British ship arriving in the Boston port was reported at a meeting among the colonists. A plan was made to deal with the crisis. Reports say that between fifty and 250 men showed up by the docks. Some of these men had hatchets. In a big mob, they stormed the docks. The men had changed their looks with coal dust and costumes to hide who they were. **5**

Stop and Think

5 Why do you think the men wanted to disguise themselves?

I think they wanted to disguise themselves because _____

_____

_____

One man who was there, George Hewes, spoke of this historic event years later. He said the men demanded the keys to the hatches from the ships' captains. With the keys in hand, they maneuvered their way down into the ships and lifted out all the chests of tea. The men used their hatchets to chop holes in the chests. That way, the chests could not just float on the water like corks. Then they tossed the chests over the sides of the ships. **6**

Stop and Think

6 What did the men do after they lifted out the tea chests?

The men _____

_____

_____

The next morning, tea was still floating on the water. To prevent it from being saved, some men beat the tea with boat paddles to make it sink. British ships were in the bay, but the men encountered no problems.

News of this event, now called the Boston Tea Party, traveled up and down the coast. Colonists at other ports did the same thing, tossing tea into the water. The battle for freedom had begun. **7**

© Harcourt

Stop and Think

7 Why is it important to know about these events?

It's important to know because _____

_____

_____

Think Critically

1. What happened in Boston in 1773? Copy the chart, and fill in the most important events. **SEQUENCE**

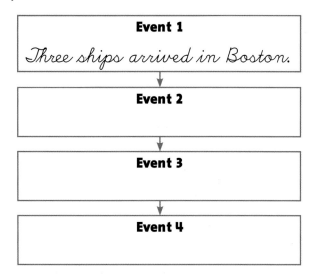

Event 1
Three ships arrived in Boston.

↓

Event 2

↓

Event 3

↓

Event 4

2. Why did the Boston colonists dump the tea? **MAIN IDEA**

The Boston colonists dumped the tea because

_____

_____

_____

3. Why did other ports start tossing tea into the water? **CAUSE AND EFFECT**

Other ports started tossing tea into the water because

_____

_____

_____

envisioned

gesture

proportion

resisted

scholars

specialized

Vocabulary

Build Robust Vocabulary

Write the Vocabulary Word that completes each sentence in the letters. The first one has been done for you.

Dear Dora,

We visited the State Capitol in Sacramento, California. I was

looking forward to seeing the tile floor that was restored in

the 1970s. Many **(1)** _____scholars_____ have said

that the floor is a work of art. I wanted to see for myself.

I had **(2)** _____ it as something grand.

It was! At first, Dan **(3)** _____ our

attempts to get him to tour the Capitol. Now he is glad he went.

I'll tell you more details in my next letter.

Your pal,
Flor

© Harcourt

Dear Dora,

Here are just a few more notes from our tour of the California State Capitol. In the 1970s, a man named Hans Scharff had to clean each floor tile by hand. He was an artist that **(4)** _____ in tile.

What a chore! He took up each tile from the floor in order to clean them one by one. Then he had to put each of the tiles back down again. The tiles had to be in the same order they had been in before. The **(5)** _____ of the tiles had to be the same, too.

It was a big job, but Scharff finished the tile floor. Then he took off the sheets in a grand **(6)** _____ , as if to show how perfect it was. I have some prints to show you when we get home. You'll be amazed!

Your pal,
Flor

THE TILE FLOOR

by Emily Hutchinson • illustrated by Shadra Strickland

The year was 1975. The State Capitol in California had been in use for more than one hundred years. It was no longer safe. The brick walls could fall down, so the problem couldn't be ignored.

The Capitol needed to be torn down or restored. It was hard to think of what to do. All who envisioned a grand State Capitol wanted to restore it. **1**

Stop and Think

1 What was the problem with the Capitol? How could it be solved?

The problem was _____

It could be solved by _____

_____

All the walls and floors had to be torn out. Then stronger ones could go in. The upper floor had more problems. The marble floor was like art. In fact, some art scholars said it was indeed art. It dated from 1906. They resisted a plan to get rid of it. How could it be saved?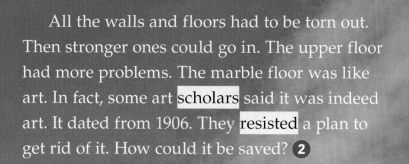

Small marble tiles covered the floor of the Capitol.

Stop and Think

2 What do you think will happen to the marble floor?

I think the marble floor will _____

_____

_____

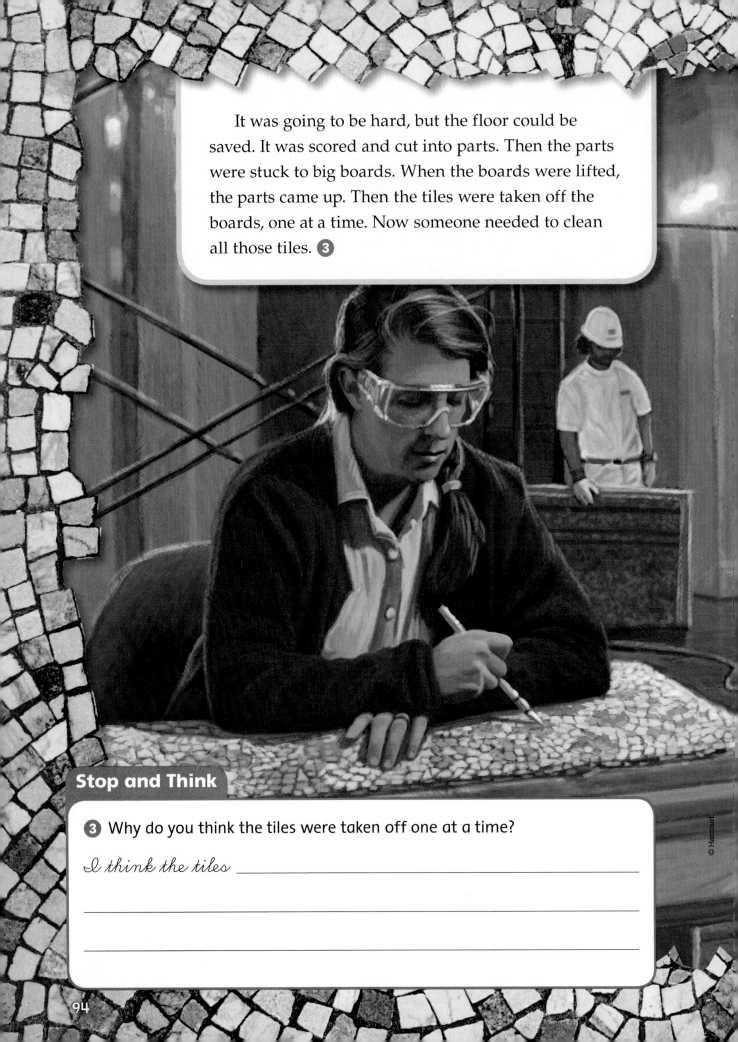

It was going to be hard, but the floor could be saved. It was scored and cut into parts. Then the parts were stuck to big boards. When the boards were lifted, the parts came up. Then the tiles were taken off the boards, one at a time. Now someone needed to clean all those tiles. **3**

Stop and Think

3 Why do you think the tiles were taken off one at a time?

I think the tiles _____

_____

_____

© Harcourt

Can you see yourself as the one who had to do all of that cleaning? The floor had hundreds and hundreds of little marble tiles, and each one was no more than one inch wide. What a chore! Hans Scharff was an artist who specialized in tile. It was his job to clean all of the tiles. Each line and corner must have taken a long time. As the days wore on, his hands must have gotten sore! **4**

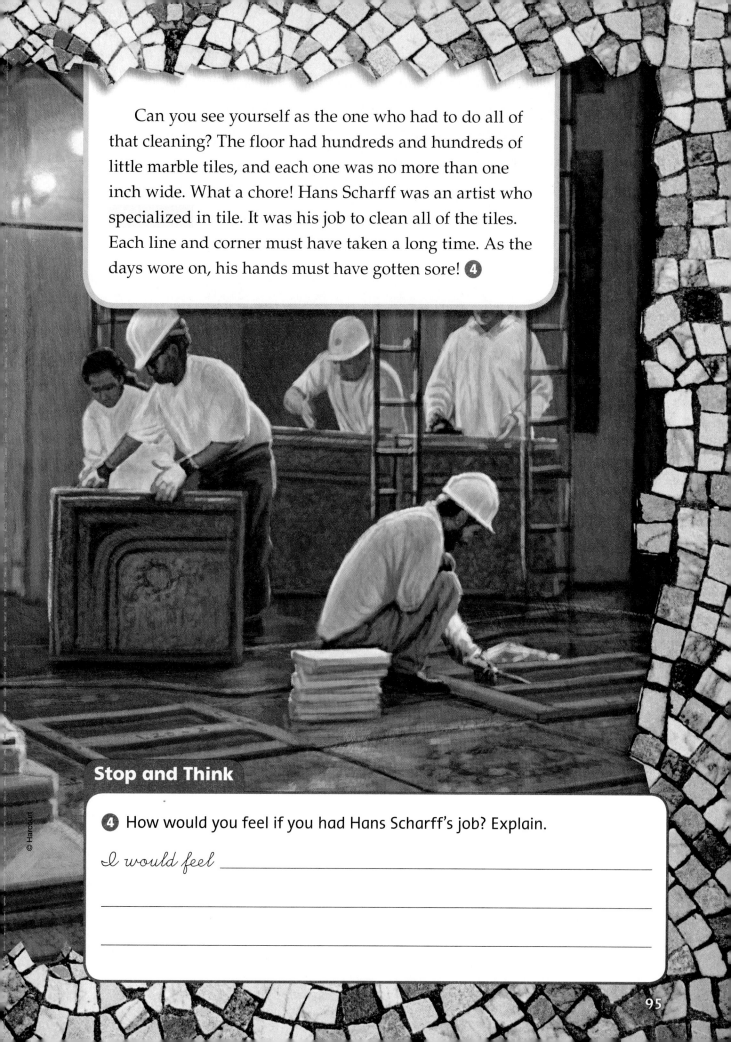

Stop and Think

4 How would you feel if you had Hans Scharff's job? Explain.

I would feel _____

_____

_____

After all that cleaning, Hans still had more chores to do. He poured paste on big sheets. He set the tiles on the paste in the same order and proportion. Then he let the paste set. These tile-covered sheets were stored in boxes. All of the sheets were sent by train back to the Capitol. It was time to complete the floor. **5**

Workers carefully cleaned and restored the marble tiles.

Stop and Think

5 What did Hans Scharff do after cleaning the tiles?

After cleaning the tiles, Hans Scharff _____

_____

_____

More was in store for those tiles! The next task was to set the tiles on the upper hall floor. When the tiles were set, off came the sheets in a grand gesture. The job was finished! At last, the marble floor was complete. **6**

Stop and Think

6 Do you think it was a good idea to restore the tile floor? Explain.

I think that _____

_____

_____

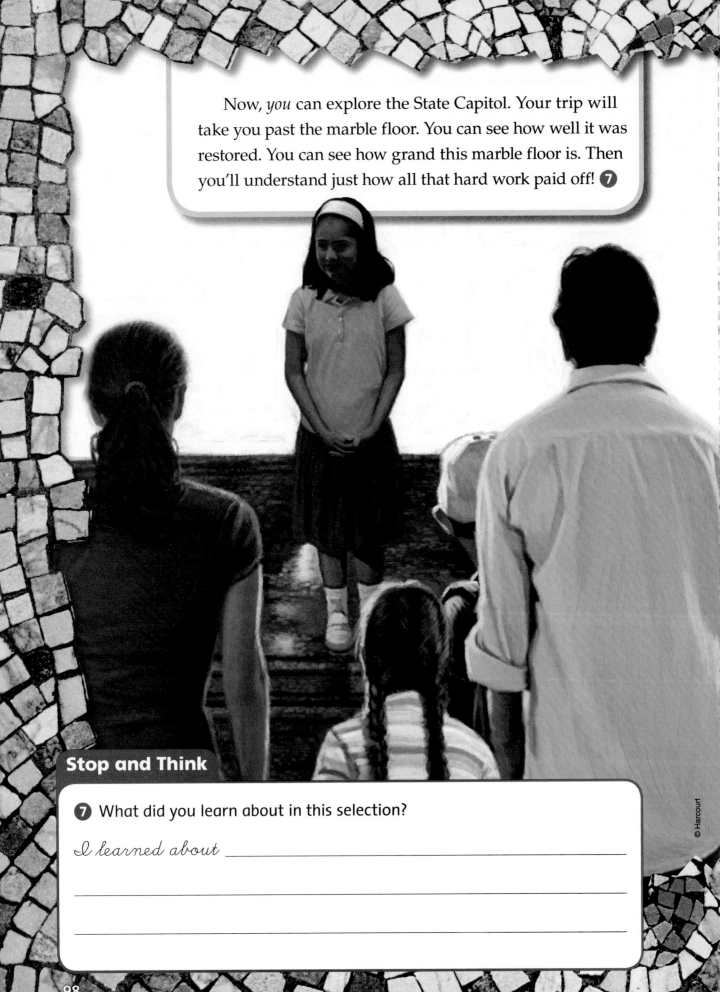

Now, *you* can explore the State Capitol. Your trip will take you past the marble floor. You can see how well it was restored. You can see how grand this marble floor is. Then you'll understand just how all that hard work paid off! **7**

Stop and Think

7 What did you learn about in this selection?

I learned about _____

_____

_____

Think Critically

1. What is the main idea of this selection? **MAIN IDEA**

   The main idea is that _____

   _____

   _____

2. What were the last steps in restoring the tile floor? Copy the chart, and fill it in. **SEQUENCE**

Event 1
The tiles were sent back to the Capitol.

   ↓

Event 2

   ↓

Event 3

3. How is the new Capitol like the old one? How is it different?
   COMPARE AND CONTRAST

   It's like the old one because _____

   _____

   It's different because _____

   _____

   _____

Vocabulary

Build Robust Vocabulary

Write the word that best completes each sentence.
The first one has been done for you.

1. Volunteers are taking calls at the

   _____**charity**_____ event to help

   destiny   charity   crisis

   hurricane victims.

2. Chef Mark appears in lots of shows like this. This

   _____ baker is the next

   grateful   raspy   eminent

   entertainer for the show.

3. Chef Mark's assistant calls. He can't come! Megan,

   Rose's assistant, is _____ .

   aghast   encountered   appealed

4. When Rose learns that Chef Mark can't come, she is

   _____ .

   inadequate   eminent   disgruntled

5. Megan and Rose are _____ . What

   crucial   dismayed   absentminded

   can they do to fill the time on the show?

6. Chef Mark can be _____ . "Did he

        absentminded   wistful   grateful

forget about our show?" asks Rose.

7. Dawn has a plan. She says she can make a

_____ with turkey.

concoction   ruckus   crisis

8. Just before going on, Dawn begins to feel

_____ . She is not sure about

crucial   raspy   inadequate

being on TV.

9. Megan tells Dawn she can do it. "Don't be

_____ !" she says. "You can

aghast   modest   disgruntled

make a good meal!"

10. In the middle of the show, Dawn can't find the pepper

she needs. She _____ the recipe

        amends   resists   proclaims

and decides to try a new plan.

Write the answer to this question. Use a complete sentence.

11. If a person is absentminded, what do they often do?

_____

_____

Hurricane Turkey

by Ernest Kaye • illustrated by Rob McClurkan

Narrator

Rose,
telethon host

Megan,
Rose's assistant

Art,
the camera operator

Dawn,
a worker

People
Watching

Narrator: We are on the set of "Hurricane Help," a telethon to raise money for victims of the last hurricane. A talented singer has just performed.

People Watching: Hurray! Yes!

Rose: Thank you. Please call now to help the victims of the terrible hurricane. This is important charity work that will help many people.

Dawn: We all need to do what we can to help. ❶

Stop and Think

❶ What do you know about telethons?

I know that telethons _____

_____

_____

Narrator: Megan looks upset as she whispers to Art.

Megan: The assistant to the eminent baker who was our next entertainer just called. He can't make it!

Narrator: Megan is aghast and has a look of panic on her face. She is waving her hands in the air to signal to Rose.

Rose: Our helpers will be here to take your calls. But first, let's hear these words from our sponsors.

Narrator: Rose, with a disgruntled look, asks Megan what's the matter. ❷

HURRICANE HE

Stop and Think

❷ Why does Megan panic?

Megan panics because _____

_____

_____

Megan: Chef Mark isn't here!

Rose: That's a bad surprise! Chef Mark can sometimes be absentminded. Did he forget about our show?

Megan: No, he's stuck in traffic.

Narrator: Dawn, one of the workers, has heard them talking.

Dawn: Don't be dismayed. I may have a plan!

Art: Is this an offer to perform?

Rose: What can you do to entertain people? ❸

Stop and Think

❸ What do you think Dawn's plan will be?

I think Dawn's plan will be _____

_____

_____

Dawn: Well, my grandma was a chef, and she showed me how to make some of her best treats. I could demonstrate how to make one.

Megan: Could you make a dinner?

Dawn: Sure, what do you have?

Narrator: Rose is back on camera, talking about help for the victims of the hurricane.

Rose: Let's show that we are the best helpers on Earth. Please call now to offer your help. **4**

HURRICANE HELP

Stop and Think

4 How is Dawn helping the hurricane victims?

Dawn is helping by _____

_____

_____

Narrator: Dawn and Megan discover some things in the back that could be used for a dinner.

Dawn: We have crackers, eggs, a turkey, and some garlic. I think I can make some concoction.

Art: Better get going! It's now or never!

Dawn: Yikes, I feel a bit inadequate. Can I do this?

Megan: Sure you can! Don't be modest; you'll do fine. **5**

Stop and Think

5 How would you feel if you were Dawn? Explain.

I would feel _____

_____

_____

Rose: We have a surprise visitor! Dawn will demonstrate how to make a simple dinner.

Dawn: Thank you. My grandma called this meal "Pepper Turkey."

Art: Let me get a close-up of the steps.

Dawn: First, I put the turkey in a bowl. Second, I cover it with beaten eggs. Third, I add lots and lots of pepper.

Rose: That looks wonderful, but I don't see any pepper.

People Watching: Yes, where is the pepper? **6**

Stop and Think

6 What steps do you take to make "Pepper Turkey"?

To make "Pepper Turkey," you first _____
_____
_____

Narrator: With a look of horror, Dawn searches for pepper. Then Rose holds up the garlic, and Megan waves a handful of crackers. Dawn thinks fast and amends what she said before.

Dawn: Umm, let's use crushed crackers and chopped garlic and call it "Hurricane Turkey." What do you say?

People Watching: Yes! Hurray!

Rose: Mmm, "Hurricane Turkey" smells wonderful.

Art: The calls are pouring in!

Rose: Well, it looks like "Hurricane Turkey" has blown everyone away! Thanks for the help, Dawn. **7**

Stop and Think

7 What lesson do you learn about working together?

I learn that _____

_____

_____

Think Critically

1. What conflicts occur in this story? PLOT

   In this story, _____

   _____

   _____

2. Why do you think Dawn offered to cook? CHARACTER

   I think Dawn offered to cook because _____

   _____

   _____

3. Do you think the telethon was a success? Why do you think so?
   MAKE JUDGMENTS

   I think that the telethon _____

   _____

   _____

broached
conducted
dignified
inflammable
rowdy
seldom
shatter

Vocabulary

Build Robust Vocabulary

Write the Vocabulary Word that completes each sentence in the postcards. The first one has been done for you.

Dear Julie,

I'm on a neat ship! My dad is teaching history to the university students. Last week, he **(1)** _____conducted_____ classes on the deck. Classes at sea are fun. We learn a lot! This morning, I learned how **(2)** _____ objects catch on fire. I'll explain it when I get back.

39¢

Julie Steel

1424 Main Street

Stamford, CT 06901

Your friend at sea,

Tony

© Harcourt

Dear Patrick,

I made some friends on the ship. Their parents are professors like my dad. There are a lot of university students on the ship, too. The older students often get wild and **(3)** _____ !
My friends and I do our best to act in a
(4) _____ way, but we still have fun.

Your friend,
Tony

Patrick Hall
737 Spring Street
Stamford, CT 06901

Dear Grandpa and Grandma,

Our ship was in a big storm. It seemed like it would **(5)** _____ the deck into tiny bits. My friend said the ship could be **(6)** _____ by big waves. The storm didn't get that bad!
Mom wants calm waters, but that
(7) _____ happens.
Write to me!

Your grandson,
Tony

Grandpa and Grandma
1516 Allen Street
Hudson Falls, NY 12839

MY HOME IS SHIPSHAPE

by Susan Blackaby • illustrated by Doug Bowles

Fifth grade turned out to be the best year of my life! My dad got a job on a ship at the University at Sea. In the program, college students apply from all over the United States to spend a year on a ship. The ship is a lot like a regular campus. It even has a library. What a way to find out what the world is like! You get a firsthand look at other lands. You learn history, which my dad teaches. You get to see amazing art up close. You can study beliefs and customs. Mom and I were so lucky! The families of the professors don't always get to go. **1**

Stop and Think

1 What can you tell about the narrator?

I can tell that the narrator _____

_____

_____

The professors and their families all bunked on one deck. Mom and Dad had a cozy cabin, and I stayed in a cabin I shared with Kyle. He came from Dallas, and his dad was teaching French. Kim was across the hallway. She came from Denver, and her mom was the math professor. The three of us really hit it off.

There were 450 college students on the trip. They lived on the decks below us. They could get pretty rowdy! We may have gotten a bit wild, too, but most of the time we did our best to act in a dignified way. **2**

Stop and Think

2 What do you learn about the characters?

I learn that the characters _____

_____

_____

At first, we all felt queasy. The ship rocked and rocked, and we didn't have our sea legs yet.

Mom told us she would like the sea to be like a sheet of glass from the ship to the horizon. Kim agreed. But the sea was seldom that still.

"These waves are puny," said Kyle. "Think what will happen if a storm hits. Ships can be broached by giant waves." We teased Kyle because he had a big case of nerves and slept in his life jacket for the first three weeks. ❸

Stop and Think

❸ How could the sea be like a sheet of glass?

The sea could _____

_____

_____

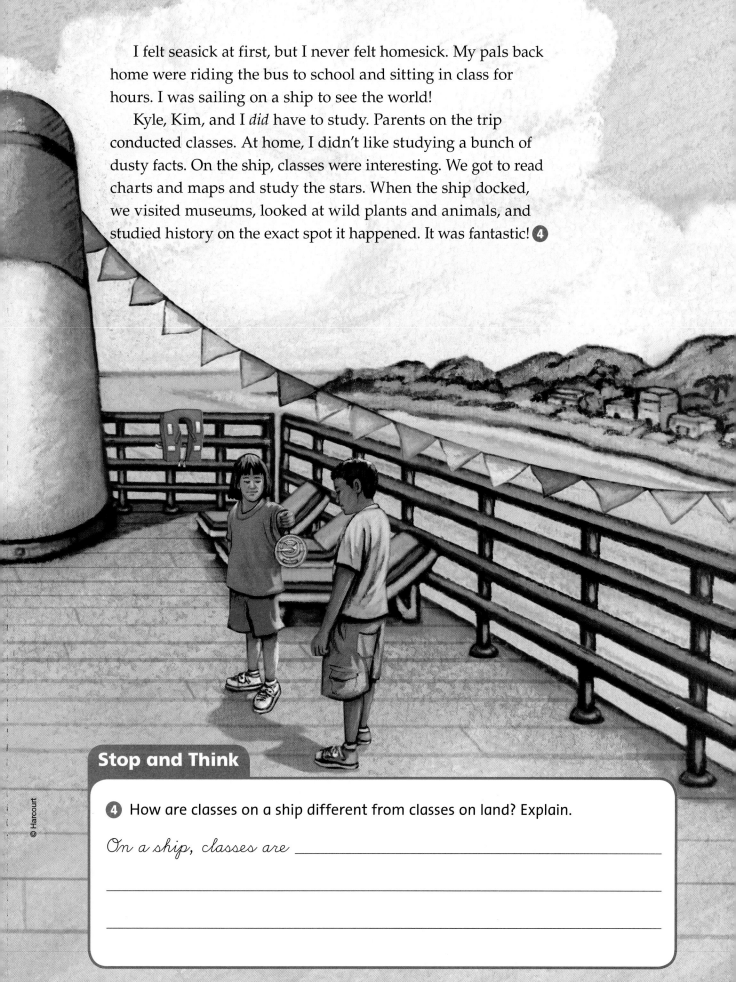

I felt seasick at first, but I never felt homesick. My pals back home were riding the bus to school and sitting in class for hours. I was sailing on a ship to see the world!

Kyle, Kim, and I *did* have to study. Parents on the trip conducted classes. At home, I didn't like studying a bunch of dusty facts. On the ship, classes were interesting. We got to read charts and maps and study the stars. When the ship docked, we visited museums, looked at wild plants and animals, and studied history on the exact spot it happened. It was fantastic! ❹

Stop and Think

❹ How are classes on a ship different from classes on land? Explain.

On a ship, classes are _____

_____

_____

Every day at sea we kept daily logs. At first we had plenty to say, but when we got used to sailing, one day at sea could be a lot like the next. We ran out of things to report.

"Friday, October ninth," said Kyle. "We're on a ship. What else?"

"All is quiet," Kim said, and turned to me. "What does your log entry say, Tony?"

"'Our home is shipshape,'" I read.

Just then, a blinding flash ripped across the sky. Thunder clapped loudly, and rain pelted the ship so hard that it seemed as if the deck would shatter into tiny bits. **5**

Stop and Think

5 What facts might you include in a daily log?

I might include _____

_____

_____

We scrambled below deck, and Mom met us at the cabins.

"Good idea to come in," she told us. "Why don't you kids just stay below? It's raining like crazy out there!"

Out of the rain, we were fine but our papers got soaked. Kyle set his soggy log by the heater. "When it gets dry, I'll have plenty to say," he told us.

"Set it a little farther over," said Mom. "It's risky to put an inflammable object like that next to the vent."

"Flames would be *big* news," said Kim. **6**

Stop and Think

6 What do you think Kyle will write in his log entry?

I think Kyle will write _____

_____

_____

When the rainstorm had passed, we went up on deck, surprised to see that the sky had cleared and the sun was shining. It was just another lazy day at sea.

"Where were we?" Kyle asked, pulling out his log entry.

"*All was quiet,*" Kim recited. We grinned at how quickly that had reversed.

"Our home was shipshape," I said, "and it still is!" **7**

Stop and Think

7 How is their home still shipshape?

Their home is still shipshape because _____

_____

_____

Think Critically

1. What happens in the story? Copy the chart, and fill it in. **PLOT**

Characters	Setting
Tony, Kyle, Kim, Mom	University at Sea ship

Plot Events

1. Tony and his pals write in their daily logs.
2.
3.
4.

2. Why does the author tell the story from Tony's point of view? **AUTHOR'S PURPOSE**

The author tells the story from Tony's point of view
because _____

_____

_____

_____

3. Why does Tony's attitude toward school change? **CAUSE AND EFFECT**

Tony's attitude toward school changes because _____

_____

_____

_____

adjust
debris
internal
pesky
recoil
residents
specimens

Vocabulary

Build Robust Vocabulary

Write the Vocabulary Word that completes each sentence in the letters. The first one has been done for you.

Dear Mom,

Summer camp here at the Sound is the best! The other

(1) _____residents_____ of my cabin are girls I know I'll get

along with. Thanks so much for sending me! The camp and cabin

are very clean—no **(2)** _____ or trash anywhere.

Mom, it's up to your standards! It will not be hard for me to

(3) _____ to being away from home. After

all, it's just for two weeks. But I'll be missing you.

Hugs and kisses,

Amy

Dear Mom,

Today my team went out to the beach. I saw some of those
(4) _____ birds that always beg us for treats. I plan to find out more about them. Maybe I'll find out how to keep them from bothering us!

Jan poked at something that looked like a flower in the water. I was surprised to see it **(5)** _____ fast and close up. I'll have to ask the program director what it is.

I spotted many crabs and other mollusks, too. Dan said that their outer shells protect their **(6)** _____ organs. That's very interesting, don't you think?

I'm looking forward to studying more of these interesting
(7) _____ the next time we go out. It's fun!

Still missing you,
Amy

121

Rock Hounds on the Sound

by Susan Blackaby • illustrated by Ute Simon

Many kids who are residents of northwest Washington have homes near the Sound. The Sound is a body of water in the top corner of the state. The Sound and surrounding shore are home to all kinds of plants and animals.

Some summer camps teach kids about the habitats of the Sound. Studying these habitats helps people understand more about the forms of life that are found there. **1**

Sound

Olympic Peninsula

• Seattle

Washington

The Olympic Peninsula is west of the Sound. The main part of Washington is to the east.

Stop and Think

1 Where does this story take place?

The story takes place _____

_____

_____

Amy Fowler and her pal, Jan, are taking part in a summer day camp. It's part of the Kitsap Outdoor Camp, held near the girls' hometown. Both girls are rock hounds, and they like to spend time outside. They decided that a camp on the Sound would be interesting and fun.

On the first day, the girls sat with the rest of the campers in the longhouse at Old Man House Park. The day was lousy. The rain came down hard. **2**

Stop and Think

2 Why do you think the girls are called rock hounds?

I think they are called rock hounds because _____

_____

_____

123

"Hello!" a tall man shouted loudly over the rain. "This is quite a crowd! My name is Dan Powers, and I'm the program director. I'm also a member of the Suquamish (Su•KWOM•ish) Indian tribe. We've made our homes on this land for thousands of years. Now it's part of Kitsap County. When we first came here, there was nothing for miles around. Now, you can see Seattle, named for our leader, on the other side of the Sound."

Dan peered out the window at the dark clouds. "Well, it was out there this morning," he joked. ③

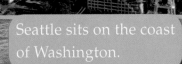

Seattle sits on the coast of Washington.

Stop and Think

③ How did the Sound look long ago? How does it look today?

Long ago, the Sound _____

_____

Today, the Sound _____

The kids giggled.

"Anyhow," Dan went on, "I hope you're all set to find out about the birds, fish, and mammals that make their homes here. We're lucky to have so many interesting plants and animals all around us." **4**

Some animals make their homes in the Sound itself. Others are found on the shore or in the forests. Wildlife shares this habitat with humans—400,000 of us!

In the past, habitats were lost as land was used to make towns. Wildlife had to adjust as the open land was used up. Now, some of the land is protected.

Stop and Think

4 What happens when humans build homes on the Sound?

When humans build homes on the Sound, _____

_____

_____

125

After the rain had stopped, Dan had the campers form teams. "Here are the ground rules," he said. "Don't pick up any specimens. Just study them and make notes about them."

Amy's team went bird watching. By the end of that first day, Amy had spotted three golden-crowned kinglets. She had found an eagle's nest, too. It looked like a mound of debris stuck in the top of a tree. Amy had also counted six kinds of gulls. She recognized the gulls as those pesky birds that always begged for picnic scraps. **5**

Golden-crowned Kinglet

Bald Eagle

California Gull

Stop and Think

5 Why is it important for the campers to follow Dan's rules?

It's important to follow Dan's rules because _____

_____

_____

On the second day, Jan and Amy's team hiked down the beach.

"Look at this thing recoil," said Jan. She poked at a flower under the water. The sea anemone snapped closed.

Then Amy found a hermit crab hidden in the sand.

"The crab uses the shell like a house," explained Dan. "It protects the crab's soft internal organs."

"He looks crowded in there," said Amy. "I think he's outgrown his shell house."

"When he needs a bigger shell, he'll get one," said Dan. **6**

Sea Anemone

Hermit Crab

Stop and Think

6 What does Amy learn about the hermit crab?

Amy learns that _____

_____

_____

On the third day, Amy's team went out on the Sound in a boat. Jan shouted excitedly when she saw a harbor seal. Otters chowed down on clams as they floated on beds of seaweed. Just as they were about to return to shore, an orca leaped up out of the sea.

"Wow!" said Jan. "I had no idea the Sound was so crowded!"

"There's wildlife all around us," said Amy. "I can't wait to find out more about everything I've seen."

"That's just what I was counting on," said Dan. **7**

Orca

Sea Otter

Stop and Think

7 What do you think Amy will do when she gets home?

I think Amy will _____

_____

_____

Think Critically

1. Why does the author tell us about the day camp? AUTHOR'S PURPOSE

The author _____

_____

_____

2. What do Amy and Jan learn about the Sound? MAIN IDEA AND DETAILS

Amy and Jan learn that _____

_____

_____

3. What animals do the girls see on the land? What animals do they see in the water? Copy the Venn diagram, and fill it in. COMPARE AND CONTRAST

Land   **Both**   **Water**

all live on the Sound

129

bellowing
betrayed
escapades
outcast
reputation
unfathomable
withered
yearning

Vocabulary

Build Robust Vocabulary

Write the Vocabulary Word that completes each sentence. The first one has been done for you.

One of the best tall tales is about the adventures of a sailor named Salty. The man was so big that he reached the skies. Many sailors like to tell stories of his **(1)** _____ escapades _____ . Salty had quite a **(2)** _____ on the high seas. He was known for being bigger than life.

Just how big was Salty? Think of a huge watermelon next to a shrunken and **(3)** _____ grape. If a normal man was the size of the grape, Salty would have been the melon.

Salty was loud, too! Before he learned to speak in low tones, his **(4)** _____ sounds scared everyone he met.

Salty often got looks of fear and spite that

(5) _____ what many were

thinking about him. Some people refused to talk to

him. Salty was an **(6)** _____ .

He wanted to be a sailor, but Salty was so big that no

ship could hold him.

Salty kept on **(7)** _____ to be

at sea. One day, Salty said he *would* sail the seas. This

was **(8)** _____ to the sailors at

the time. How could he fit on any ship?

Then Salty had a huge ship made just for him.

After that, he lived a sailor's life!

Write the Vocabulary Word that best completes the synonym web.

9.

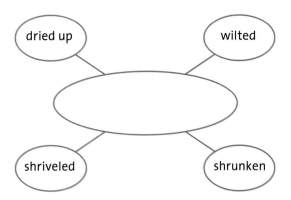

Salty on the High Seas

by Susan Blackaby
illustrated by Jill Newton

Are you yearning for a good story? If you travel near any port in the world, keep your ears open for tall tales. The best ones tell of the escapades of a sailor named Salty. Salty had quite a reputation on the high seas. He was bigger than life. In fact, he was as big as a grizzly bear on the night he was born. As a grown man, Salty was so big that he used a ship's oar to pick his teeth!

As a sailor, Salty was something of an outcast. He was so big that no ship could hold him. ❶

Stop and Think

❶ Why is Salty bigger than life?

Salty is bigger than life because _____

_____

_____

So Salty had a huge ship made just for him. He steered that ship, *Bright Courser,* right around the world. In every port, he made a big splash.

On one trip, the ship sat stalled off the coast of a mighty land mass because the wind refused to blow. At that time, South America and Africa formed one continent.

After three weeks without even a slight breeze, the sailors longed for the sight of the winds filling the sails. Among sailors, this lack of wind was called "the doldrums." **2**

Stop and Think

2 What causes the doldrums?

The doldrums are caused by _____

_____

_____

"We need a big breeze so that we can get going," Salty said. "I'm supposed to be in India right now. Bags of nutmeg and pepper are piled high on the dock. I hate being tied up here night and day."

All of a sudden a light bulb went on in Salty's brain. "All hands on deck!" he cried. Salty's bellowing shout broke glass from Florida to Bombay. "I have a way to fight these doldrums! If there's no wind, we'll make our own." ❸

Stop and Think

❸ Why does Salty need to reach India?

Salty needs to reach India because _____

_____

_____

The first mate frowned, and his look of fright betrayed what the rest were thinking. Salty might be hatching one of his wild plans.

"What do you have in mind, sir?" he asked.

"I'll huff and I'll puff and I'll blow this ship right over the land if I have to," Salty cried.

The men were frightened. Then the first mate gave a slight nod. "That might work. But start slow and just give a light sigh. After all, a blast from you could be a disaster." ④

Stop and Think

④ Why are the men frightened?

The men are frightened because _____

_____

_____

Salty waved his hand as if batting away flies.

"Stop fussing. A fine, soft puff is all it will take. Then we'll need one big breeze to set us right."

"Sir, I think we just need a light puff."

"Nonsense," said Salty. He breathed in and gave out a sigh. The sail fluttered like a bird in flight. Men scrambled to their posts high in the ropes. Salty sniffed. He snorted. And then a very big, bad thing happened.

Salty sneezed. **5**

Stop and Think

5 What do you think will happen next?

I think that _____

_____

_____

The ship ripped across the water, and it didn't stop when it hit the beach. It split the mighty land mass in two! Salty and his men held on tight as jungle and then grassland skidded by. The sea flowed in to fill the rip.

"I've never seen such a sight!" cried the first mate, who was withered like a dried plant from the big breeze.

"Excuse me," said Salty. "It must have been all that pepper from our last trip. But I was right! We might be in port by nightfall." ⑥

Stop and Think

⑥ What happens after Salty sneezes?

After Salty sneezes, _____

_____

_____

A sailor on the dock met *Bright Courser* when it arrived in India. He was shocked to see Salty and his crew.

"Where did you come from?" he asked. "You're early!"

"We took a short cut," said the first mate.

"Yes," said Salty. "We nosed our way in. By the way, we formed a new continent and tripled the size of the Atlantic."

"That's unfathomable!" said the sailor.

"Not for Salty," said the first mate. "Just hold on tight if he sneezes." 7

Stop and Think

7 Why does the author use the phrase "nosed our way in"?

The author uses this phrase because _____

_____

_____

Think Critically

1. What happens in the tall tale? Copy the story map, and fill it in. **PLOT**

Characters	Setting

Plot Events

1. *Salty's ship is stuck in the doldrums.*
2. *Salty sneezes.*
3.
4.

2. As a sailor, Salty's size causes many problems. How does he react to these problems? **CHARACTER**

Salty reacts by _____

_____

_____

3. How can you tell that this is a tall tale? **AUTHOR'S PURPOSE**

I can tell this is a tall tale because _____

_____

_____

139

accumulate

elastic

elongates

intricate

replenishing

rigid

underlying

vanish

Vocabulary

Build Robust Vocabulary

Write the Vocabulary Word that completes each sentence in the selection. The first one has been done for you.

Without water, life on our planet would not be possible. All life, from simple organisms to the most

(1) _____ intricate _____ ones, depend on water.

The amazing thing about water is that it exists in three states. When it gets very cold, its molecules slow down. Then it becomes **(2)** _____ and frozen. This is water's solid stage. When energy from the sun warms the frozen water, it melts. This is its liquid form. When it gets hot, the water will turn to steam and

(3) _____ . You may not see water in this gas form, but it's there. It's in the air around you as water vapor.

Water is **(4)** _____ , which means it can stretch out. You can see this as you watch a drop of water sliding down a window pane. It **(5)** _____ , or becomes longer, as it moves.

Water is found everywhere. In its liquid form, it can **(6)** _____ in large puddles after a rain. In its frozen form, it can fall to make layer upon layer of snow. Each **(7)** _____ layer is frozen water.

The water supply on our planet stays the same. It changes forms, but the supply is always **(8)** _____ itself. When the rains come, our creeks and rivers swell, and much of it finds its way back to the sea.

WATER ON OUR PLANET

by Susan Blackaby   illustrated by Gary LaCoste

Water flows under bridges. It rages down rivers and plunges over waterfalls. It crashes in giant waves on the beach. It splashes over a large part of our planet. Out of the tap, it may not seem like a big deal. After all, it's clear. It has no smell. It has no taste. And yet without it, life on our planet would not be possible. In fact, water is what gives our planet the edge. **1**

Water is called H_2O. It's made up of two hydrogen atoms and one oxygen atom. The plus and minus charges attract.

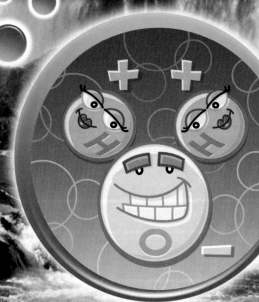

Stop and Think

1 What do you already know about the importance of water?

I already know that _____

_____

_____

Like all things, water is made up of molecules. Most liquids tend to flatten out to make a film. The way the atoms in a water molecule are arranged makes the molecules clump together. They form rounded drops. A drop is a very small amount of water. However, it has a huge number of molecules.

What makes water so amazing? For one thing, water exists in three states. When water freezes, the molecules slow down and get rigid. This is water's solid stage. Energy from the sun heats up the frozen water. It turns into a liquid. When it gets hot, water turns to steam, which is a gas. **2**

Stop and Think

2 What causes water to turn from a solid to a liquid?

Water turns from a solid to a liquid when _____

_____

_____

Water molecules clump together to form drops. The drops are sticky. They stick to glass, cloth, and even this page of paper.

Water is elastic. Think about how a drop drips down a window pane. It begins as a small, round ball. Then it changes shape. As it slides, it elongates. It stretches into the shape of a teardrop. It keeps stretching until it is like a large ribbon. Then the ribbon splits apart. New drops form. These new round drops begin to stretch and slide down the glass. **3**

Water drops slide down windows like ribbons, sometimes splitting apart.

Stop and Think

3 What happens when water drips down a window? Summarize.

When water drips down a window _____

_____

_____

A lot of the things that water can do seem like strange magic tricks. It can seep into small cracks and creases. It can travel up a wick. It can edge up the sides of a glass. It can travel up the stem of a plant to reach the leaves.

Water can carve out a rock ledge on a cliff. It can act like a giant dredge to create a gorge or canyon. When it rains, water can accumulate to make a gigantic puddle. Then it will vanish when the sun comes out. **4**

Stop and Think

4 What do you think causes the water to vanish?

I think that _____

_____

_____

Where does the water in the puddle go? It evaporates, or changes to vapor. Water molecules float in the air in the form of gas. They stick to things that are cold and condense, or turn back to liquid. For example, drops will form on the outside of a cold drink glass.

In the morning, you can see that water in the air has settled on the grass, trees, and bushes. If it's cold outside, the water will form frost. When the sun shines, the water changes back to vapor. **5**

Stop and Think

5 Why does water settle on grass at night?

Water settles on grass at night because _____

_____

_____

The water supply on our planet stays the same. The molecules keep changing, but the supply is always replenishing itself. Most of the water is stored in the sea. It heats up and evaporates. The vapor rises. Then it hits cold air. The molecules stick together. They make clouds. The clouds drift over the land. Some of the water molecules fall to the ground. Raindrops swell creeks. They send rivers raging back to the sea. Intricate snowflakes fall on peaks. The peaks store an underlying layer of frozen water. **6**

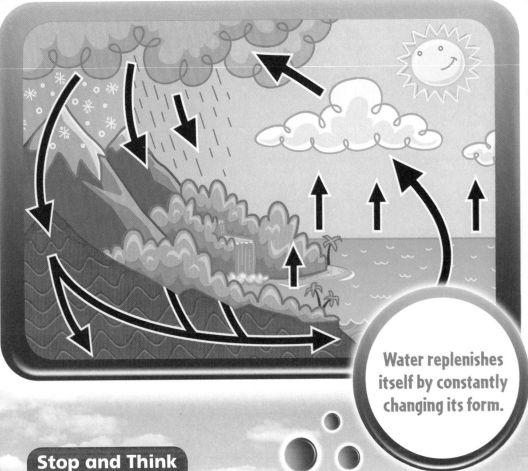

Water replenishes itself by constantly changing its form.

Stop and Think

6 What happens after water vapor hits cold air?

After water vapor hits cold air, _____

_____

_____

Think about water the next time you weed your garden, play soccer on wet grass, or plunge into a cold lake. Water molecules are all around you, and they're on the go. The water in your bean plants may have been in a puddle on a street in Germany! The water soaking into your sneakers may have been frozen in a high ridge. The water drop on the tip of your nose may have lapped at the edge of a warm beach. When it comes to water, stranger things have happened! **7**

Stop and Think

7 How do you think the author feels about water?

I think the author feels that _____

_____

_____

Think Critically

1. What causes water to evaporate? Copy the organizer, and fill it in. **CAUSE AND EFFECT**

Cause		Effect
	→	*Water evaporates.*

2. How does our water supply stay the same? **MAIN IDEA AND DETAILS**

Our water supply stays the same by _____

_____

_____

_____

3. Compare the three stages of water. How are they different? **COMPARE AND CONTRAST**

Here is how they are different: _____

_____

_____

_____

Vocabulary

Build Robust Vocabulary

Write the word that best completes each sentence.
The first one has been done for you.

1. Grandma tells the children a tale about Crow. She wants to

_____**recount**_____ the tale about how Crow found

recoil   recount   shatter

daylight for the Inuit.

2. Grandma says, "In his _____ to

                 endeavor   specimen   escapade

spice things up for the Inuit, Crow would tell them stories."

3. Crow talked about a time when the land was so dark that it

was _____ . Nothing could live there.

  rigid   teeming   uninhabitable

4. Then Crow found a place where the sun was always

shining. The sky was _____ with light.

             rowdy   bellowing   brimming

5. In this place of sun and light, the land was

_____ with life. Birds

teeming   monotonous   pesky

filled the sky.

© Harcourt

6. Crow found the daylight in a golden box. He wanted

to bring it back to the Inuit to make their boring and

_____ life more fun.
unfathomable   monotonous   intricate

7. Sunshine would be a blessing for the Inuit, but too much

would make the land dry and _____ .
elastic   sorrowful   parched

8. Grandma says, "The land where the Inuit

_____ used to be dark all year. Can
dwell   recount   recoil

you imagine that darkness in your world?"

9. Grandma's story makes the past life of the Inuit sound

sad and _____ .
intricate   sorrowful   parched

10. Grandma's words _____ us until
recount   accumulate   sustain

she gets to the best part of the story!

Write the answers to these questions. Use complete sentences.

11. If someone asks you to recount a story, what does that person want you to do?

_____

_____

12. If a place is teeming with life, what is it like? Describe what you would see there.

_____

_____

GRANDMA'S TALE

Adapted from an Inuit Story

by Susan Blackaby • illustrated by Kyle M. Stone

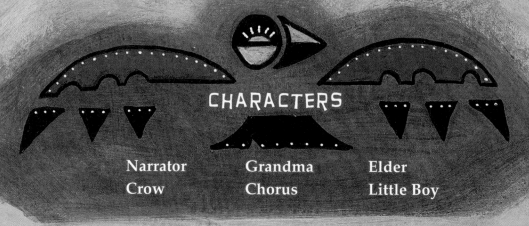

CHARACTERS

Narrator   Grandma   Elder
Crow   Chorus   Little Boy

Narrator: It's December in the far northern lands where the Inuit dwell. Grandma is telling tales to pass the time.

Grandma: Ages ago, it was dark all year long. Life followed a monotonous cycle of darkness following darkness. Crow tried to spice things up by telling stories.

Crow: I fly long distances across the sky. In places, the land is so dark that it's uninhabitable. No one could survive there. But where the sun shines, spruce trees grow so tall they slice holes in the sky. ❶

Stop and Think

❶ Why does Crow tell stories?

Crow tells stories because _____

_____

_____

Grandma: The people wanted Crow to recount his tales over and over. Because they dwelled in a place of ice and darkness, they found these tales exciting.

Crow: The sun sparkles like ten thousand stars. The sky is brimming with light and teeming with birds.

Grandma: The Inuit wanted this daylight.

Chorus: Please bring this light to our dreary, dark world!

Grandma: Crow followed the streams to the rim of the sea.

Narrator: Grandma flapped her arms like magnificent wings. **2**

Stop and Think

2 How is the sun like ten thousand stars?

The sun is like ten thousand stars because _____

_____

_____

153

Grandma: As Crow approached, the world burst into color, painted by that artist, the sun. Then, the village princess passed by.

Crow: That girl is approaching the lodge of the elder. I think this person keeps the daylight safe. My endeavor is to enter his lodge without being seen. I will use my powers to do this.

Grandma: Crow shrank to the size of a speck of dust. Then he drifted down and clung to the girl's cape as she entered the lodge. Right away he spotted a fancy golden box. **3**

Stop and Think

3 What do you think will be inside the box?

I think that _____

_____

_____

Crow: I was right! The daylight *is* hidden in this place.

Grandma: A small boy played by the fire. Tiny Crow slipped into the boy's ear.

Narrator: As Grandma tells this tale, she rubs her ear with fierce strokes, just as the boy would have done.

Grandma: The boy began to tug at his ear and fuss.

Elder: Little man, why are you fussing?

Grandma: Crow whispered in the boy's ear.

Crow: Say that you want to play with a sunbeam.

Little Boy: I want to play with a sunbeam. ❹

Stop and Think

❹ Why does the boy rub his ear?

The boy rubs his ear because _____

_____

_____

Grandma: The elder reached into the box and pulled out a droplet of sunshine. He tied it to a piece of string and then handed it to the boy.

Elder: Here you are. Look at it dance! It's like a puppet!

Grandma: Crow fluttered, and the boy fussed again.

Elder: Little man, what's the matter?

Grandma: Crow whispered in the boy's ear.

Crow: Say that you want to race on the beach.

Little Boy: I want to race on the beach.

Elder: Then let's take the sun outside. **5**

Stop and Think

5 Why does Crow want the boy to go outside?

Crow wants him to go outside because _____

_____

_____

Grandma: The instant they were outside, Crow dove at the boy's hand, grasped the piece of string, and flew away. Before long, the Inuit saw a streak of yellow race across the sky. It flickered over the waves.

Crow: Look at the prize I got for you!

Grandma: As Crow dropped the sunbeam, it broke into hundreds of pieces, in every color. The Inuit were startled and amazed by the sparkling colors.

Chorus: The world is lit up like a rainbow! ❻

Stop and Think

❻ How is the Inuit's land different now?

The land is different now because _____

_____

_____

Crow: I only grabbed one tiny sunbeam. You must use it for only part of the year, so it won't get used up. And don't use too much of it, since it can make your land dry and parched.

Grandma: The Inuit raced the sun across the sky. They danced and sang, celebrating the gift of daylight.

Chorus: Thank you, Crow! Now the darkness won't make us sorrowful. Our memories of the sun will sustain us in the dark months.

Grandma: Now, for the Inuit, dark winter is followed by the glorious light of the sun. **7**

Stop and Think

7 Why must the Inuit use daylight for only part of the year?

They must use it for only part of the year because _____

_____

_____

Think Critically

1. What is the problem in the story? How is it resolved? **PLOT**

The problem is that _____

_____

It's resolved when _____

_____

_____

2. Why do you think Crow brought back the daylight? **CHARACTER**

I think that Crow _____

_____

_____

3. Do you think Crow did the right thing? Explain. **MAKE JUDGMENTS**

I think that _____

_____

_____

baffled

essence

indication

insights

instinct

proposed

tempted

Vocabulary

Build Robust Vocabulary

Read the story and think about the meanings of the words in dark type.

"Why are you so annoyed?" Leslie asked Joyce. Leslie was **baffled.** She didn't know why Joyce was so upset.

Joyce explained that she was mad at her brother, Roy. Roy never gave any **indication** that he was proud of her. It seemed that he always felt **tempted** to call his sister Slowpoke. Roy didn't think Joyce was a fast runner.

"That's crazy, Joyce!" said Leslie. "You're the **essence** of an all-around athlete. You work so hard. In fact, I know you'll win your next race." Leslie had an **instinct** for these things.

Leslie liked to write for the paper at Westpoint Academy. She came up with a plan for an article to go on the sports page. In the article, she would share some **insights** about the track team. She wanted Roy to admit that his sister was a star runner.

Leslie **proposed** the plan to Joyce. It involved a nice joke on Roy. Joyce smiled, "I think I'm going to enjoy this," she said.

**Write the answers to these questions. Use complete sentences.
The first one has been done for you.**

1. What is a different way of saying, "Leslie was **baffled**"?

Leslie was confused or puzzled.
_____

2. "It seemed that he always felt **tempted** to call his sister Slowpoke."
What does this sentence mean?

_____

_____

3. What would be an **indication** that Roy is proud of his sister?

_____

_____

4. What will Leslie be doing when she shares **insights** about the
track team?

_____

_____

5. What does Leslie seem to think is the **essence** of an athlete?

_____

_____

6. What do Leslie's **instincts** tell her?

_____

_____

7. What is a different way of saying, "Leslie **proposed** the plan to
Joyce"?

_____

_____

© Harcourt

TEAMWORK

by Susan Blackaby • illustrated by Erica Pelton Villnave

Each morning, when Roy gave his sister a ride to Westpoint Academy, he said the same thing as Joyce got out of the car.

"See you later, Slowpoke!" he'd call.

It was starting to bug her. Joyce had joined the track team, just like Roy. She was training hard, and Coach Doyle did *not* think she was a slowpoke. But Roy hadn't seemed to notice this.

"Why are you so annoyed?" asked Leslie, Joyce's pal, as they walked to class.

"It's Roy," sighed Joyce. "He doesn't think I can run!" ❶

Stop and Think

❶ Why is Joyce annoyed with Roy?

Joyce is annoyed because _____

_____

_____

"Hmm, what would you think if I proposed a little joke?" said Leslie.

"Roy is the sports editor on *The Point*, isn't he? I'll submit some articles about the team. I'll make up a nickname for you and rave about your talents. Roy will be baffled because he won't know it's you. Once he finds out, he'll realize that you're a star runner."

Joyce smiled. "I think I'm going to enjoy this," she said. **2**

Stop and Think

2 Why does Joyce like Leslie's plan?

Joyce likes Leslie's plan because _____

_____

_____

"You'll have to run fast," Leslie pointed out. She put up her hand for a high five. "You perform your job well, and I'll do mine."

Later, Leslie explained her plan to Joyce's pals on the track team.

"From now on, Joyce is undercover. Her new identity is SJ. It stands for Sprinting Joyce. Don't tell Roy."

"Your secret is safe with me," Meg said, and Rita agreed. **3**

Stop and Think

3 Why does Leslie say that Joyce must run fast?

Leslie says that Joyce must run fast because _____

_____

_____

© Harcourt

Leslie's story was in *The Point* the next week.

☆ SPORTS ☆

SJ Makes Tracks

by Leslie Chin

You can hear the buzz from Main Street to Sandpoint. What is all the noise about? Let me share my insights. Our girls' track team is setting a swift pace that may take them all the way to the top. The rising star is SJ.

"With her speed and stamina, she's leading the team. She is the essence of an all-around athlete," said Rita Arroyo. **4**

HOME 40
AWAY 38

Stop and Think

4 What insights does Leslie share in her story?

Leslie _____

_____

_____

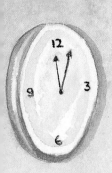

"Boy," said Joyce with a grin. "I *have* to win now. You left me no choice."

"Don't worry," said Leslie. "I have an instinct for these things. Just run. Don't give Roy any indication of how fantastic you are. Act as if you can barely keep up."

Just then, Roy walked by their table. "Who is this SJ?" he asked.

"You must be kidding!" Meg exclaimed. "Everybody knows SJ." ❺

Stop and Think

❺ Is Leslie's plan working? How do you know?

Leslie's plan _____

_____

_____

166

Leslie's next article was big news.

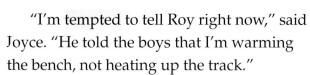

☆ SPORTS ☆
Coach Doyle Predicts Victory
by Leslie Chin

Westpoint, get set for a big win! Our girls' track team may be the next state champs, and we have SJ's blazing feet to thank.

Coach Doyle is predicting victory. "There is every indication that SJ will take us to the top," she said.

So join us on Saturday and enjoy the fun!

"I'm tempted to tell Roy right now," said Joyce. "He told the boys that I'm warming the bench, not heating up the track."

"Just run," said Leslie. **6**

Stop and Think

6 What do you think will happen next?

I think that _____

_____

_____

At the track meet, Joyce didn't disappoint Leslie. In fact, she led the relay team to a big win. While Joyce was getting her ribbon, Leslie joined Roy in the front row.

"How about a quote on SJ—short for Sprinting Joyce?"

Roy grinned. "How about this for a quote? 'I'm boiling mad, at myself, for not supporting my sister!'"

Later, the team helped Leslie create a headline for her final story. Rita voted for 'Winning Team Sheds Tears of Joy!' But Joyce preferred 'Winning Team Gets Cheers from Roy!' **7**

Stop and Think

7 What does Roy learn about respecting others?

Roy learns that _____

_____

_____

© Harcourt

Think Critically

1. How does the author use Leslie's articles to move the plot forward? Copy the story map, and fill it in. **PLOT**

Characters		Setting

Plot Events

Article 1:

Article 2:

2. Why is running fast so important to Joyce? **CHARACTER**

Running fast is so important because _____

_____

_____

3. How does Roy feel at the beginning of the story? How does he feel at the end? **COMPARE AND CONTRAST**

At the beginning, Roy feels _____

_____

At the end, Roy feels _____

_____

169

embarked
extravagant
gourmet
hiatus
precarious
throng
unimaginable

Vocabulary

Build Robust Vocabulary

Write the Vocabulary Word that completes each sentence. The first one has been done for you.

Shawna did not want to visit Gran's farm. To her, life on the farm was too boring. But her mom said to regard it as a **(1)** _____hiatus_____ from her normal chores. So Shawna **(2)** _____ on the trip she didn't want to take.

Shawna hauled her bag off the plane. There was a **(3)** _____ of people waiting for passengers. When Uncle Paul saw Shawna, he commented on how tall she was. He asked if it affected her dancing. Shawna giggled and said, "My two-step is kind of **(4)** _____ . I wobble all over the place."

At supper, Gran served up **(5)** _____

treats. Shawna liked Gran's strawberry shortcake the best.

Then everyone wanted to hear ten thousand details about

the family. Shawna realized that she was having fun!

After two rainy days, Shawna was no longer having

fun. Aunt Dawn said that so much rain at this time of year

was **(6)** _____ . "This is the wettest

August I've ever seen!" she exclaimed. Then Uncle Paul got

out an awesome chess set. Each piece had been carved by

hand with **(7)** _____ care.

Write the Vocabulary Word that best completes the synonym web.

8.

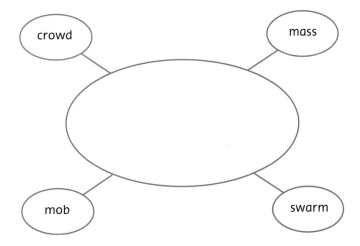

Rained Out at Gran's

by Juanita Jeffrey • illustrated by Jason Wolf

The last thing Shawna wanted to do was spend a week at the farm with Gran, Aunt Dawn, and Uncle Paul. She tried to change her mom's mind. She reasoned and begged, but her mom wouldn't budge.

"Think of it as a hiatus," said Mom. "You won't have to mow the lawn or help with laundry. It'll be a holiday." **1**

Stop and Think

1 How does Shawna feel about visiting Gran's farm?

Shawna feels _____

_____

_____

Shawna didn't say so, but she felt a little shy with Aunt Dawn and Uncle Paul. She hadn't seen them for a long time. She felt like she didn't know them at all.

"It'll be awful," Shawna said. "There's nothing to do there but watch the clock tick."

"Don't be silly!" said her mom. "August is the perfect time for a visit. The peaches are ripe, and the fish are just begging to be caught. You can go hiking or swim in the lake."

Shawna sighed. She would just have to face her fears. **2**

Stop and Think

2 What can you tell about the setting at Gran's? Underline the words that tell you this.

I can tell that the setting _____

_____

_____

Three days later, Shawna hauled her bag off the plane. She saw Uncle Paul in the throng, waving his straw hat like a flag.

"Hello there, missy," Uncle Paul called out. "You've grown six inches since I saw you last. Must make it hard to dance."

Shawna giggled. "My two-step *is* kind of precarious," she said. "I wobble all over the place."

At supper, Gran served up one gourmet treat after the next, including strawberry shortcake. Everyone wanted to hear ten thousand details about the family. When she crawled into bed that first night, Shawna had to admit she was having fun. **3**

Stop and Think

3 What does her family do to make Shawna feel welcome?

Shawna's family makes her feel welcome by _____

_____

_____

The next day, it started raining. Rain came down in buckets, filling up the lakes and streams and spilling over. On the second rainy day, Shawna stared out the window. She felt awful. All of this rain was washing away her plans for fishing, hiking, and swimming.

"This is unimaginable," said Aunt Dawn. "It never rains like this in August. This is the wettest August I've ever seen!"

Uncle Paul set a box and a chessboard on the table. "Do you play chess?" he asked Shawna.

"No," said Shawna, watching her uncle open the box. ❹

Stop and Think

❹ What do you think will happen next?

I think that _____

_____

_____

Then, Shawna's jaw dropped. The chess set was awesome. Each piece had been carved by hand with extravagant care. The pawns were baby animals such as fawns, bunnies, kittens, and cubs. The bishops were beavers sitting on their back legs. The kings were giant toads about to spring. The queens were swans. Set up, the board was an enchanted forest. ❺

Stop and Think

❺ How is the board like an enchanted forest?

It's like an enchanted forest because _____

_____

_____

"Where did you get this awesome chess set?" asked Shawna. She picked up a piece shaped like a hawk with curved claws.

"I made it on wet days," said Uncle Paul. "After all, there's not much to do here when it rains." He then embarked on a long, involved speech about the game.

Gran could see that Shawna was confused by all of these new rules. "Make a drawing to show her which way each piece can go on the board," she suggested. ⑥

Stop and Think

⑥ Why does Uncle Paul explain the game to Shawna?

Uncle Paul explains the game because _____

_____

_____

During the rainy week, Shawna and her uncle played game after game. They also worked on a chess set of her own. Shawna decided to make all the pieces look like members of her family.

When it was time to leave, Uncle Paul said, "You come back, now. I always need someone to beat at chess."

Shawna hugged Dawn. Gran said, "I hope you'll be back when it isn't raining."

Shawna smiled. "I'll be back, rain or shine," she said. "And I'll bring my new chess set. With King Paul on the board, I simply can't be beaten!" **7**

Stop and Think

7 What does Shawna learn about trying new things?

Shawna learns that _____

_____

_____

© Harcourt

178

Think Critically

1. How does Shawna change her mind about the farm? Copy the story map, and fill it in. **PLOT**

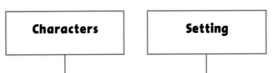

Characters	Setting

Plot Events

1. *Shawna doesn't want to go to the farm.*

2. *At the farm, it starts to rain.*

3.

4.

2. What effect does the rain have on Shawna's visit?
   CAUSE AND EFFECT

   The rain causes _____

   _____

   _____

3. How does Shawna feel about her family now? **CHARACTER**

   Shawna feels _____

   _____

   _____

compartments

invasion

phobia

swayed

vetoed

wispy

Vocabulary

Build Robust Vocabulary

Read the story and think about the meanings of the words in dark type.

Dennis got teamed up with Marla and Nina for the Biology Fair. He would have **vetoed** such a partnership if he could have. He didn't really want to work with those two. They wanted everything to be just perfect.

Marla and Nina wanted their project to be about Dutch Bantam chickens. Marla knew a lot about them. The team met at Marla's. She showed them the chickens and explained how they nest in separate **compartments** in a henhouse. Dennis held a chicken in his lap as Marla told him more. The chickens didn't seem to care about the **invasion** of their space. They just kept on pecking for seeds and clucking to one another. Their **wispy** tails looked like dainty little fans.

The girls suggested that Dennis narrate a slideshow for the fair. He objected strongly. Dennis had a **phobia** about speaking in public. The last time Dennis had been in front of an audience, the room had **swayed** and he had almost fainted.

Write the answers to these questions. Use complete sentences. The first one has been done for you.

1. What did Dennis want to **veto**?

Dennis wanted to veto being partnered with Marla and

Nina for the Biology Fair.

2. Why does a henhouse have separate **compartments**?

_____

_____

3. What kind of **invasion** do you think would disturb chickens?

_____

_____

4. Besides a chicken's tail, what might be **wispy**? Describe it.

_____

_____

5. How is Dennis affected by a **phobia**?

_____

_____

6. When the room **swayed**, what did it look like to Dennis? How did he feel?

_____

_____

Dennis the Chicken Man

by Susan Blackaby
illustrated by Red Hansen

Mr. Goodwin told the students in his class to count off to form teams for the Biology Fair. Dennis could not believe he wound up with Marla and Nina.

"I *would* get teamed up with those two," he said to Brooks at lunch. "They always have to be so perfect."

"Look, I wish I could help you out, pal," said Brooks. "But that's just the way it goes sometimes. You'll do fine."

Just then, Nina and Marla came up to discuss the project. **1**

Stop and Think

1 Why is Dennis upset?

Dennis is upset because _____

_____

_____

"We think we should do a report and media show on chickens," said Marla. "I raise them for 4-H, and my Bantams are used to being shown."

"We can meet at Marla's on Saturday," added Nina. "We'll show you her hens, okay?"

"Meeting celebrity chickens would fulfill my boyhood dream," said Dennis.

"Don't be sarcastic," Marla said. "Chickens are so misunderstood." ②

Stop and Think

② What do you learn about Nina and Marla?

I learn that _____

_____

_____

Saturday, Dennis cradled a hen in his lap while Marla told him all about the birds. The chickens amazed him. They were small and elegant. Their wispy tails stood out like dainty fans.

"Bantams came from the Dutch East Indies," explained Marla. "Spice traders kept them on their ships so that they would have eggs to eat. Bantams have been popular in Holland for hundreds of years. They first came to the United States around 1950."

By the time Marla was finished, Dennis was hooked. **3**

Stop and Think

3 What are some facts that Dennis learns about Bantams?

Dennis learns that Bantams _____

_____

_____

Over lunch, the three mapped out a plan.

"I'll make a giant poster with an egg-laying time line," said Nina. "I can explain the cycle step-by-step."

"Good," said Marla. "I'll construct a model of a wooden henhouse. It can have three compartments. We can bring a hen with us and show how the nesting boxes look."

Dennis piped up. "I can reproduce some maps and drawings and create a slideshow about their history." **4**

Stop and Think

4 What do the three students plan to show in their presentation?

They plan to show _____

_____

_____

"This will look so good," said Nina. "I can manage the slideshow while Dennis narrates."

An uneasy Dennis began to fidget in his seat. "Umm, can't the slideshow just speak for itself?" he asked.

Marla vetoed this idea. "The judges would rather hear a speech than look at a slideshow by itself."

Unfortunately, Dennis had an extreme phobia when it came to public speaking. He had to get out of this! **5**

Stop and Think

5 Why is Dennis uneasy?

Dennis is uneasy because _____

_____

_____

186

On the day of the fair, Dennis made one final heroic effort to ditch the speech, but Marla and Nina insisted. As he stood on stage, frozen stiff, the room swayed. He couldn't even look at the audience.

"I don't feel so well," Dennis whispered to Marla.

Marla whispered back, "Then I'll just have to *egg* you on." She waited for him to giggle, but he just stood there and shook. Marla tried again. "You *hatched* this performance. What's the matter, are you *chicken?*" **6**

Stop and Think

6 Why does Marla tell Dennis chicken jokes?

Marla tells Dennis chicken jokes because _____

_____

_____

Dennis felt the invasion of butterflies in his stomach flutter away. Marla stood alongside him, providing support. "I'm here if you faint, Chicken Man."

"Thanks," he said. "I think I'm good to go. Let's begin."

Nina clicked on the first slide, showing a white egg.

"Good morning," said Dennis. His voice shook a little. He took a second to adjust and relax. Then he began.

"Which came first, the chicken or the egg?" **7**

Stop and Think

7 How do you think the presentation will go? Explain your answer.

I think the presentation _____

_____

_____

188

Think Critically

1. What happens in the story? Copy the story map, and fill it in. PLOT

Characters	Setting
Dennis, Nina, Marla	school, home

Plot Events
1. Dennis is paired with Nina and Marla.
2.
3.
4.

2. Why does the author use the title "Dennis the Chicken Man?"
   AUTHOR'S PURPOSE

   The author uses this title because _____

   _____

   _____

3. How is Dennis different at the end of the story? COMPARE AND
   CONTRAST

   At the end of the story, Dennis _____

   _____

   _____

   _____

device

feat

industry

irrepressible

prestigious

tendency

Vocabulary

Build Robust Vocabulary

Write the Vocabulary Word that completes each sentence in the advertisements. The first one has been done for you.

Stick with Super Glue!

Dr. Harry Coover has an **(1)** ___irrepressible___ inventing spirit. He's been at it again! We just can't stop him! Not long ago, Coover was working on a **(2)** _____ to be used for one thing, but he made something else. He invented a terrific glue. We call it super glue! Try it and you'll see just how super this glue is. Everything sticks with super glue!

This Glue Is Super!

Are you in the habit of thinking that glue never works like it should? Do you have a **(3)** _____ to think it might not hold? Try super glue and your glue problems will be over. It can hold two steel beams together, with two men hanging on! What a **(4)** _____ ! You must try this product!

Need Glue?

The glue **(5)** _____ does not give out awards. But if it did, our product would get the most **(6)** _____ award possible. That's because super glue is like no other! Try it and you'll see!

Stick with Us

The Story of Harry Coover and Super Glue

by Nathaniel Craig

How many times have you used glue? You may have used the gooey stuff ever since you were little. There are all kinds of glue. There is glitter glue, colored glue, and even "super" glue.

Most people who try super glue have a tendency to use it again and again. You might think inventing super glue was quite a feat. Not so! Super glue was invented almost by mistake. **1**

Stop and Think

1 What do you already know about super glue?

I already know that _____

_____

_____

For many years, people have found ways to get things to bind, or stick together. Before modern glue was invented, we stuck things together with honey, eggs, and tree sap. Just try to make a model plane using eggs. What a mess!

Inventors came up with glue in England in 1750. It was first made from fish! Later, glue was made out of rubber, animal bones, milk, and, finally, human-made liquids. Even now, inventors are trying to find new ways to make better glues. ❷

Stop and Think

❷ What do you learn about the first glues?

I learn that _____

_____

_____

Sometimes an inventor is looking for one thing but discovers—out of the blue—something quite different. That's what happened with super glue.

Dr. Harry Coover was born in 1919 in Delaware. He went to Cornell University to study. Coover had always enjoyed trying new ideas. By 1942, he was working in a lab testing all kinds of plastics for a device used by the military. One kind of liquid he tested turned out to be too sticky. "Everything I was working with stuck to everything else," Coover later said. **3**

Dr. Harry Coover

Stop and Think

3 Why was the liquid's stickiness a problem for Coover?

The liquid's stickiness was a problem because _____

_____

_____

However, Coover didn't have time to investigate this new substance. He finished the project for the military and went on to a prestigious job testing new mixtures and compounds in the camera-making industry.

In 1951, Coover was trying to make a safer canopy for jet planes. A worker on his team tested different ways to make the plane tops. In one test, he put a small bit of a liquid between two pieces of glass. It was the same sticky liquid Coover had worked with years before. ❹

Stop and Think

❹ What do you think happened to the glass?

I think that _____

_____

_____

Just as you might have guessed, the pieces of glass stuck together. The worker tried prying the pieces apart, but he couldn't do it. They just would not budge.

Dr. Coover knew that this was nothing new. Years before, he had seen for himself just how sticky this stuff was—what a nuisance! But then he began to pursue the idea. "What we had," Coover said, "was a new super glue." **5**

In 1957, some glue company employees tested the new glue by hanging a car from a crane with just one drop of super glue. It worked!

Stop and Think

5 How did Coover react to the problem?

Coover _____

_____

_____

In 1958, after seven years of testing, Coover's super glue was offered for sale. Coover went on TV to show just how sticky his glue was. He told the host of a popular show that just one drop of the glue would hold him up. Coover joined two steel beams with one drop of glue. The host hung from the bottom beam. Then Coover did, too! After this, super glue was a big hit.

Coover's glue has been used in many ways. One form of his super glue is a benefit to everyone. It stops bleeding in an instant by sealing up wounds and is used in surgery in place of stitches. **6**

Stop and Think

6 How is super glue a benefit to everyone?

Super glue is a benefit to everyone because _____

_____

_____

Coover's inventing spirit was irrepressible. He registered more than 460 patents for different discoveries, not just for super glue. In 2004, he was elected to an American inventors' hall of fame.

With super glue, Coover took a problem and turned it into a new tool. So, some day if you're doing something that causes problems at first, don't just toss it away. *Stick* what you've learned aside. You might be able to use it later! **7**

Coover won many awards for his work on different projects over the years.

Stop and Think

7 What do you learn from Coover about dealing with problems?

I learn that _____

_____

_____

Think Critically

1. What details help you determine the main idea? Copy the organizer, and fill it in. **MAIN IDEA AND DETAILS**

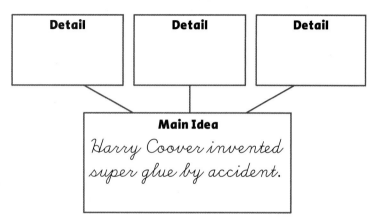

Detail	Detail	Detail

Main Idea

Harry Coover invented super glue by accident.

2. How does this selection inform you? **AUTHOR'S PURPOSE**

This selection informs me by _____

_____

_____

3. What might have happened if Coover had not pursued the idea of super glue? **CAUSE AND EFFECT**

I think that _____

_____

_____

Paste

Vocabulary

Build Robust Vocabulary

Write the word that best completes each sentence.
The first one has been done for you.

1. At the Museum of Modern Industry, the students are

   expected to behave in _____**appropriate**_____ ways.

   portable   appropriate   wispy

2. They are not permitted to play music or any

   _____ games.

   fickle   gourmet   portable

3. Loud talk or _____ play is not

   boisterous   practical   unimaginable

   allowed in the museum.

4. At the Design Lab, students are invited to invent something

   _____ to make their lives better.

   measly   wispy   practical

5. Students are asked to _____

   propose   circulate   protrude

   around the room, looking for the right tools to use.

6. Each student _____ the room to see
             scours   indicates   protrudes

what they want to try next.

7. Jessie has just one _____
                measly   gourmet   fickle

toolbox at home. The museum has a lot!

8. Mr. Knox tells his students to pick one idea and stick to it.

"Don't be _____ ," he urges.
           portable   irrepressible   fickle

9. Jessie looks puzzled. Mr. Knox makes the

_____ that Jessie has a
tendency   deduction   phobia

problem with his plan.

10. Andy works on an idea for a backpack. "I need

to get this right. I don't want my baseball bat to

_____ from my backpack!"
protrude   circulate   embark

Write the answers to these questions. Use complete sentences.

11. Name a practical item. Why is this item practical? _____

_____

12. How does boisterous play look and sound? _____

_____

DESIGN LAB
FIELD TRIP

by Susan Blackaby • illustrated by Sheree Boyd

CHARACTERS

Narrator • Robin • Mr. Knox • Andy
Jessie • Director • Intercom

Narrator: Mr. Knox is taking his class on a field trip to the Museum of Modern Industry's Design Lab. He pauses at the entrance to the museum.

Mr. Knox: I expect appropriate conduct from all of you. Remember, we all represent Wright Academy.

Narrator: The museum director meets them by the welcome sign. ❶

Stop and Think

❶ What is a synonym for "*modern*"?

A synonym for modern is _____

_____

_____

© Harcourt

Director: Welcome to the most amazing place in town! Prepare to test your inventing powers. Here, you can wrap your minds around a job designed to test your thinking.

Narrator: The class follows the director upstairs to a huge workroom while a computerized voice lists some rules.

Intercom: Portable games or music may not be played. Boisterous play or loud talk is not permitted. No knocking down displays. ❷

© Harcourt

Stop and Think

❷ What do you think the class will do next?

I think the class will _____

_____

_____

205

Director: This is our Design Lab.

Mr. Knox: This is where you get to invent practical things to make daily life better.

Narrator: The students start to circulate from workbench to workbench. They look at all of the tools and gadgets. Each student scours the room to see what they want to try next.

Andy: Check out this robotic arm! The wrist turns all the way around.

Robin: These computers have design programs. We can make 3-D pictures of our ideas! **3**

Stop and Think

3 How do you think the students feel about the design lab?

I think the students feel _____

_____

_____

Jessie: At home, we have just one measly toolbox. My dad would flip if he saw this many wrenches in one place.

Narrator: Mr. Knox talks about ways to do the assignment.

Mr. Knox: It might help if you write down three good ideas, and then pick the one that you like the best. Don't be fickle. Choose one idea and stick to it. Narrow down the choices, and then iron out all the wrinkles.

Robin: Ironing wrinkles gives me an idea!

Narrator: Robin starts drawing plans for a wrapper to keep shirts and blouses neat on closet hangers. ❹

Wright Is All Right

Stop and Think

❹ What are the students doing at the lab?

The students are _____

_____

_____

Mr. Knox: Andy, you look knee-deep in notes.

Andy: I'm going to design a backpack that can hold books and sports stuff. This pocket will hold an ice pack. My own backpack gets soaked every time I try to carry cold water.

Mr. Knox: Can you also design a sling for your baseball bat so that it doesn't protrude out of your backpack? Work on that little problem.

Narrator: Mr. Knox turns to Jessie. He sees that Jessie is looking a bit puzzled. **5**

Stop and Think

5 What does Andy like to do? How do you know?

Andy likes to _____

_____

_____

Mr. Knox: From the look on your face, I can make only one deduction. You're stuck.

Jessie: Well, I want to design a tub that scrubs itself clean.

Mr. Knox: You can't knock that idea! I'd take two, one upstairs and one down. What seems to be wrong with your plan?

Jessie: Well, this brush sits on the rim of the tub like a wreath. It starts to scrub when you turn the knob. But I can't figure out how to pour the cleaner.

Mr. Knox: You can figure it out, Jessie. Keep thinking. ⑥

Stop and Think

⑥ Why is Jessie stuck?

Jessie is stuck because _____

_____

_____

Narrator: A few students knock over a display of tools.

Intercom: No knocking over displays!

Narrator: Mr. Knox asks the students to share their designs.

Robin: I made my design into a complete closet helper.

Andy: I designed a number of backpacks for different sports.

Jessie: My invention has knee pads and a sponge wringer.

Director: I can see that you know just what to do in the Design Lab. Good job, students!

Intercom: The Design Lab is closing now. Please exit to the left and come again soon. **7**

Stop and Think

7 If you could visit a design lab, what would you invent?

I would invent _____

_____

_____

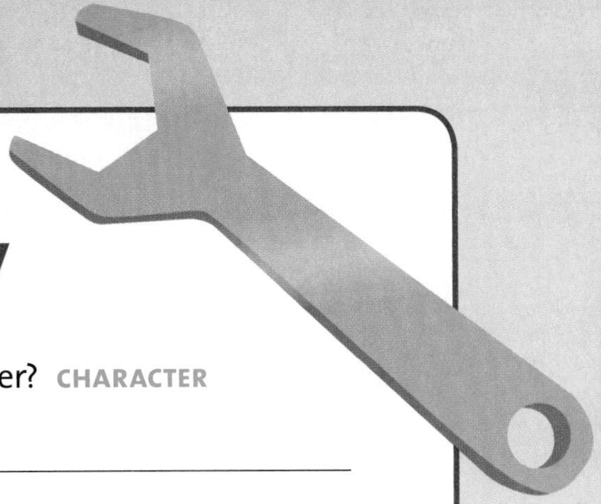

Think Critically

1. How can you tell that Mr. Knox is a good teacher? CHARACTER

Mr. Knox is a good teacher because _____

_____

_____

2. What happens at the end of the story? PLOT

At the end of the story, _____

_____

_____

3. What do the students learn about inventing? AUTHOR'S PURPOSE

They learn that _____

_____

_____

analyzing

basking

damage

detect

sleek

vital

Vocabulary

Build Robust Vocabulary

Write the Vocabulary Word that completes each sentence in the letters. The first one has been done for you.

Dear Crystal,

Yesterday, I went with my mom to a meeting about frogs. The speaker, Dr. Janet Phillips, told us how she has been

(1) _____analyzing_____ data about frogs. She does this

to find out why the frogs are having a hard time surviving.

She said that when we harm the land, we hurt the frogs, too.

When we **(2)** _____ habitats, we make it hard for

them to survive.

Next weekend, Mom and I will go out to the wetlands at night.

We'll count the frogs we see and hear. Do you want to come with us?

Your pal,

Carlos

Dear Crystal,

My trip with Mom out to the wetlands was amazing! We were able to **(3)** _____ all kinds of frog sounds. We even heard a bullfrog! At one point, I noticed a **(4)** _____ green shape that streaked across the water. It had to be a frog because there are no fish there.

I wish you could have gone with us, Crystal. It was very exciting.

Your pal,
Carlos

Dear Crystal,

I've been thinking about frogs for days. Do you remember years ago, when we saw a lot of frogs **(5)** _____ in the sun? I want to see that again. That won't happen unless we take steps to protect their habitats.

It's very important for us to take care of the land. I'm going to start telling everyone how **(6)** _____ it is. Would you like to help me?

Your pal,
Carlos

Can You Hear the Frogs?

by Brad Lewis
illustrated by Pam Johnson

To Carlos, it seemed a little phony, but he went with his mother to the meeting anyway. She said her boss's nephew had attended last week and liked it. At this meeting, they'd be taught how to hear frogs, something that Carlos believed he already knew how to do.

Dr. Janet Phillips started the meeting by saying she had been analyzing data on the number of frogs in towns around Chicago. Dr. Phillips pointed at a bar graph. The graph looked like steps going down. Carlos could see the frogs were having a hard time surviving. ❶

Stop and Think

❶ What does the bar graph show?

The bar graph shows _____

_____

_____

Dr. Phillips said amphibians like frogs are delicate. How well they survive can tell us a lot about our habitats. Helpers all over the world were keeping a count of frogs. Meetings like this were the first phase. Everyone would find out about the frogs, and then they could help with the count.

Carlos had heard enough. He wanted to be part of this. He wanted there to be more frogs basking in the sun. He took notes while the room rang with trills and croaks. Dr. Phillips was playing frog calls on a tape recorder. **2**

Stop and Think

2 What has Carlos learned about frogs so far?

Carlos has learned that _____

_____

_____

Carlos left the meeting holding a frog-counting kit that had maps, charts, and photos of different frogs. Dr. Phillips had marked ten wetlands spots for him to visit.

The next evening was just right for frog counting, damp and warm with no wind. Carlos and his mother piled into the car and drove out to find the wetlands on their map. The next phase had begun.

On the trip, they played a tape of frog sounds. Twangs and chirps filled the car. "Frog tunes!" Carlos joked, and they both laughed. **3**

Stop and Think

3 Why do Carlos and his mother play a tape of frog sounds?

They play the tape because _____

_____

_____

They found seats near the muddy pond Dr. Phillips had marked as a prime spot to detect frog songs. They took care not to damage the land. They had to be very still and quiet.

Later, Carlos saw a sleek streak of green and heard a *plop!* It must have been a frog, because Dr. Phillips said there were no fish here. Fish eat frog eggs and tadpoles. Soon a phantom foghorn sounded from the middle of the pond. "Bullfrog," Carlos whispered, and he put it down in his log. His mother nodded, chuckling softly. ❹

Stop and Think

❹ What do you think might happen if they damage the land?

If they damage the land, then _____

_____

_____

215

Carlos and his mother visited five spots that night. They were about to leave for home, when Carlos sat back down and put his finger to his lips. He had heard a quacking call. The quacks came faster and faster, from a log nearby. It might be a wood frog, and wood frogs were rare.

His mother pointed to the tape recorder in his pack, so Carlos grabbed it and held up the microphone. The frog's music went on and on. He hoped the microphone was capturing all of it. **5**

Stop and Think

5 How do you think Carlos feels?

I think Carlos feels _____

_____

_____

The following day, Carlos and his mother took their tape to Dr. Phillips. Dr. Phillips played the tape and put some numbers on a graph, then she made a phone call. Carlos and his mother both heard the phrase, "no laughing matter." They exchanged looks. Did they do something wrong?

When Dr. Phillips hung up the phone, she was frowning. She asked Carlos if he was positive the tape recorder's microphone worked. Carlos told her he knew the microphone worked because he had tested it himself. **6**

Stop and Think

6 What do you think will happen next?

I think that _____

_____

_____

"Our graphs tell us that the number of frogs in that pond is going down too fast," Dr. Phillips said. "It's vital that we find out what's going on.

"However, that tape you made is a real trophy. I'm convinced that it's a wood frog." Dr. Phillips smiled. "If so, the town will have more reason to take care of that pond and save all the frogs. You've done a good deed, Carlos."

And to think Carlos expected that meeting to be phony! His feeling of triumph couldn't be more real. **7**

Stop and Think

7 How do you think the author feels about frogs?

I think the author feels _____

_____

_____

Think Critically

1. What happens in the story? Copy the chart, and fill in the Summary column. **PLOT**

Ideas	Summary
• Carlos attends a meeting on frogs. • Carlos and his mom count frogs at a pond. • They record frog sounds and take it to Dr. Phillips. • They learn that the frogs are in danger.	

2. Now that Carlos has found a rare wood frog, how do you think other frogs will be affected? Explain. **CAUSE AND EFFECT**

I think that other frogs will _____

_____

_____

_____

3. What do you think the author wants you to learn from this story?
AUTHOR'S PURPOSE

I think the author wants me to learn _____

_____

_____

_____

cumbersome

deflated

enraptured

enterprising

monopolize

somberly

stammers

Vocabulary

Build Robust Vocabulary

Write the Vocabulary Word that completes each sentence. The first one has been done for you.

Milena is unhappy each time she has to cross Elm Street.

She looks **(1)** _____somberly_____ down the street,

waiting for a pause in traffic so she can cross.

When Milena gets to Will's house, she is still nervous

and out of breath. She **(2)** _____ a

little as she complains about the problem on Elm Street.

Will thinks that they are two **(3)** _____

fifth-graders who can get the city to put in a crosswalk.

© Harcourt

Milena and Will come up with a plan to get a crosswalk put on Elm Street. This project might **(4)** _____ all their time for a while, but it will be worth it.

The next day, they tell their teacher what they want to do. Their teacher is **(5)** _____ by their plan. "Wow! That's terrific!"

After school, Milena and Will are on the sidewalk beside Elm Street. They each have a **(6)** _____ backpack full of books on their back. They have homework to do, but they stop off to try and get some support from other residents. They find that no one wants to help them with their plan. They feel **(7)** _____ .

Write the Vocabulary Word that best completes the synonym web.

8.

delighted

entranced

enchanted

thrilled

Elm Street Speaks!

by Margie Sigman • illustrated by John Haslam

CHARACTERS

Milena, *a fifth-grade girl* **Mr. Steadman,** *a teacher*

Will, *a fifth-grade boy* **Amy Wong,** *a resident*

Officer Simms, *an officer of the law*

Stop and Think

1 How do you know that this is a play?

I know that this is a play because _____

_____

_____

ACT 1

SETTING: *Inside a residence on Elm Street.*

TIME: *The present.*

MILENA: *(Walks through the door, shaking a sodden umbrella.)* The weather is lousy out there! It took me forever to cross Elm Street, as usual. It's like crossing the runway of a big-city airport! We need a crosswalk, *now!*

WILL: We've been saying that for months. Let's do something meaningful, instead of just complaining.

MILENA: Like what?

WILL: The kids on Threadtree Lane demanded their own park. They wrote letters to the newspaper editor and the city council. It took a lot of effort, but now they have a terrific community park.

MILENA: Well, I'm ready to try anything. **2**

Stop and Think

2 What is the problem on Elm Street?

The problem is that _____

_____

_____

ACT 2

TIME: *Three days later.*

SETTING: *A fifth-grade classroom.*

MR. STEADMAN: Are you two making steady progress with your Elm Street project?

MILENA: *(Looking deflated.)* I can't convince one person in this community to produce a letter demanding a crosswalk.

WILL: I bet Milena and I talked to a hundred Elm Street residents!

MR. STEADMAN: Did you compose a letter yet?

MILENA: I already started mine. *(Begins reading from a paper.)* "My name is Milena Garza and I'm in fifth grade. Every day I face extreme danger from heavy traffic on my own street!" **3**

Make Elm Street Safe with a Crosswalk!

Stop and Think

3 What problem do Milena and Will face?

The problem is that _____

_____

_____

MR. STEADMAN: That's a fantastic beginning, Milena.

WILL: (*Slaps his forehead.*) I almost forgot! I had a major brainstorm last night while I was watching TV. What Milena read is fine, but there's a better way for us to spread the message about Elm Street!

MILENA: (*Looking puzzled.*) What do you mean?

WILL: In here's our secret weapon! (*Picks up a heavy, cumbersome backpack and reveals a video camera.*)

MR. STEADMAN: A video! What a great idea! ❹

Stop and Think

❹ How do you think the video camera will be used?

I think that _____

_____

_____

225

ACT 3

TIME: *The next afternoon.*

SETTING: *On a sidewalk on Elm Street. MILENA is standing next to AMY WONG. WILL is holding the camera steady.*

MILENA: Amy, I just saw you running across Elm Street. I don't want to monopolize your time, but we are trying to get a crosswalk installed on this street. What do you think?

AMY: *(Clutches her chest as she catches her breath.)* I think that's a fantastic idea. Should crossing the street be a life or death trip? This traffic is frightening!

MILENA: Thank you very much for your time, Amy. *(Speaks somberly in a deep voice.)* Amy Wong won't feel safe until the authorities install a crosswalk here. Okay, cut, Will! **⑤**

Stop and Think

⑤ Why is Amy so out of breath?

Amy is so out of breath because _____

_____

_____

ACT 4

TIME: *The next day.*

SETTING: *Back in the classroom.*

WILL: *(Sounding excited.)* Yesterday after breakfast we started to film. The weather was sunny and pleasant, so we were lucky.

MILENA: Will already got several awesome shots of the heavy traffic on Elm Street. There was a steady line of people wanting to talk to us, too.

OFFICER SIMMS: *(Surprising the students.)* May I interrupt? Hi, I'm Officer Simms. Mr. Steadman told me about your video. You kids have been working hard! I bet you're the most enterprising fifth graders in Featherton. We've had three accidents on Elm Street this year, so I'm more than ready to support your efforts. **6**

Make Elm Street Safe with a Crosswalk!

Stop and Think

6 What happened yesterday to make Will excited?

Yesterday, _____

_____

_____

227

WILL: *(Stammers a little with excitement.)* We have kids, moms, and dads telling their own stories on film.

OFFICER SIMMS: When you finish up your video, let's head to city hall. No one will believe what you've done. We're going to spread the word and get some things changed in this community, thanks to you.

MILENA: *(Enraptured.)* Wow! Elm Street speaks!

(Lights fade and a spotlight comes up on the Elm Street banner.) **7**

Make
Elm Street
Safe with a
Crosswalk!

Stop and Think

7 How do you think the author feels about the role of kids in a community?

I think the author feels that _____

_____

_____

Think Critically

1. What happened in the play? Copy the chart, and fill in the Summary column. **PLOT**

Ideas	Summary
• Milena and Will want a crosswalk on Elm Street. • They can't convince people to write letters. • They interview people crossing Elm Street. • Officer Simms agrees to help them.	

2. How did using the video camera affect events in the story? **CAUSE AND EFFECT**

Using the video camera caused _____

_____

_____

3. What would you like to change in your community? How can you help make this change happen? **PERSONAL RESPONSE**

I would like _____

_____

To help make this happen, I can _____

_____

_____

assuage

bustles

desolate

fervor

gouges

immaculate

Vocabulary

Build Robust Vocabulary

Read the story and think about the meanings of the words in dark type.

April was thrilled to find the perfect puppy. As the little beige and black puppy tugged at her pants leg, April made her choice. She named the puppy Buttons and took him home. But within eight days, Buttons was causing problems. The **immaculate** home that April's family had enjoyed was now not so great. "Buttons **gouges** my shoes," complained April's mom. "And he breaks vases!"

Trying to **assuage** her mom, April apologized for the puppy. She promised to try to get Buttons to behave. Each time April saw Buttons doing something bad, she spoke to him with **fervor,** but he kept doing all those things.

The next morning, April woke up to a quiet room. Where was the little puppy who always **bustles** around the room as April wakes up? He was nowhere to be found.

Feeling **desolate,** April scoured the neighborhood looking for Buttons. Her mom helped her, but they had no luck. Where could Buttons have gone?

Write the answers to these questions. Use complete sentences. The first one has been done for you.

1. Describe an **immaculate** home. What is it like on the inside?
   It is very neat and clean.
   _____

2. What is the puppy doing to the shoes when he **gouges** them?

   _____

   _____

3. Imagine you had a puppy that ruined someone's shoes. What is a good way to **assuage** that person?

   _____

   _____

4. If April speaks to Buttons with **fervor,** what might she say?

   _____

   _____

5. What do you think Buttons is doing as he **bustles** around the room?

   _____

   _____

6. How does a person feel if they are **desolate**?

   _____

   _____

The Quiet Neighbor

by Brad Lewis • illustrated by Lee White

At the Puppy Place, puppies bounced in the air, throwing their weight at April. At long last, April's mom had decided that April would take good care of a pet. They had stopped by their neighbor's puppy shelter to pick out the lucky pup. When one with beige and black spots grasped and tugged on her pants leg, April knew she had found her Buttons.

Eight days later, April wasn't so certain this arrangement was going to work out. ❶

Stop and Think

❶ Why do you think April is no longer certain about having a puppy?

I think that _____

_____

_____

"April, Buttons is at it again!" cried April's mom. She held out one of her comfy, beige shoes, pointing at deep gashes on the heel. "Look! He gouges every single shoe!"

"Sorry!" April said, trying to assuage her mother. "Great, just great," she muttered, scowling at the tumbling pup.

Buttons just always seemed to be breaking things. He chewed on shoes and knocked over heirloom vases, causing an uproar around the house. Buttons's way of slurping up spills made for an immaculate kitchen floor, but the problems far outweighed this one benefit. ❷

Stop and Think

❷ What annoying things does Buttons do?

Buttons _____

_____

_____

Buttons's talent for breaking things was an annoying habit. But that night, April forgave her frisky pup as he settled his weight on her lap and fell asleep. He looked so cute when he was dozing, and April just couldn't stay mad at him for long.

The next morning, April lay in bed waiting for Buttons's yips to wake the neighborhood. But instead she heard only silence.

"Buttons!" April bellowed at the top of her voice, expecting a fur ball to slam into her bed like a crashing freight train at any moment. ❸

Stop and Think

❸ How might Buttons be like a crashing freight train?

Buttons might _____

_____

_____

But no excited barks responded to April's call, and no fur ball scurried onto her bed. After a quick tour around, April realized that the puppy wasn't in the house. She stepped outside and saw Mrs. Ramirez hanging sheets to dry.

"Mrs. Ramirez often bustles around the neighborhood when her great-grandchildren visit," April told herself. "Maybe she's seen Buttons." Mrs. Ramirez's great-grandchildren were a loud and energetic bunch. When they weren't there, Mrs. Ramirez seemed lonely. But April's quiet neighbor hadn't seen Buttons. **4**

Stop and Think

4 How does Mrs. Ramirez feel when her great-grandchildren aren't there? Why?

Mrs. Ramirez feels _____

_____

_____

© Harcourt

April's mom helped April scour the neighborhood for the little beige and black puppy, but with no luck.

"Come on," her mother said. "Let's break for lunch. Then we'll try again."

April tried hard to rein in her feelings, but she was afraid that something terrible had happened. "I've been yelling at him a lot," she realized. "What if he's run away?"

The thought of Buttons, alone and hungry, made April desolate. **5**

Stop and Think

5 Why does April think Buttons might have run away?

April thinks Buttons might have run away because _____

_____

_____

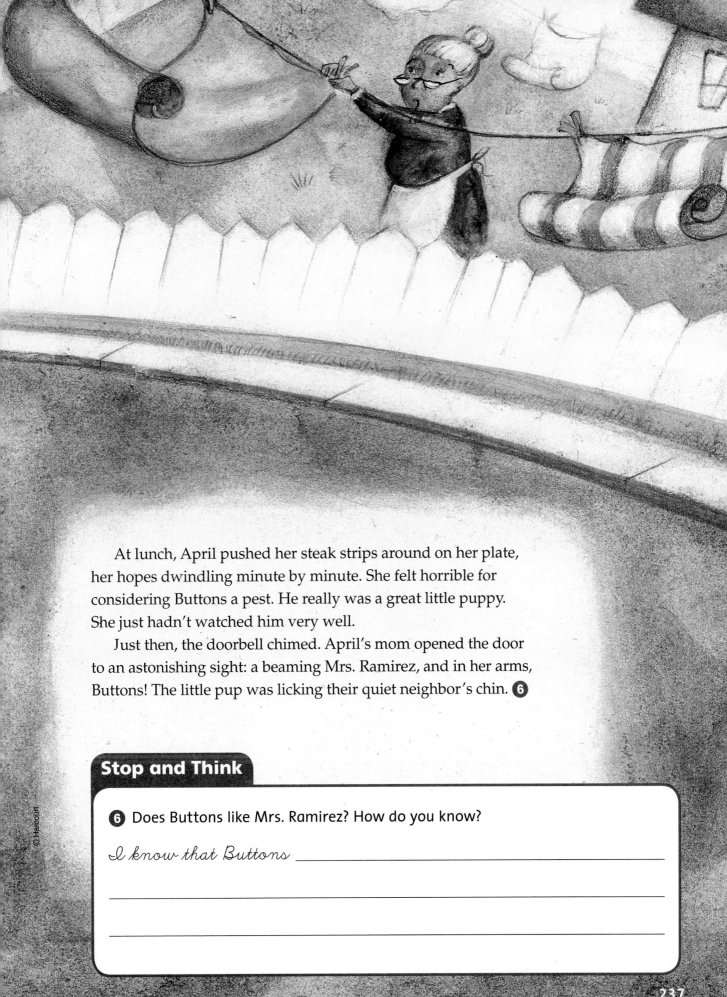

At lunch, April pushed her steak strips around on her plate, her hopes dwindling minute by minute. She felt horrible for considering Buttons a pest. He really was a great little puppy. She just hadn't watched him very well.

Just then, the doorbell chimed. April's mom opened the door to an astonishing sight: a beaming Mrs. Ramirez, and in her arms, Buttons! The little pup was licking their quiet neighbor's chin. **6**

Stop and Think

6 Does Buttons like Mrs. Ramirez? How do you know?

I know that Buttons _____

_____

_____

"Thanks, Mrs. Ramirez!" said April, with fervor in her voice. Then she noticed that Mrs. Ramirez looked happy. April realized that this was a golden opportunity to solve her puppy woes.

"Would you like a part-time puppy?" she asked.

"What do you mean?" replied Mrs. Ramirez, with interest.

"We can share Buttons! I need help watching him, and you might enjoy the companionship."

"And Buttons would like your great-grandchildren," April's mom added. "Just think of all those shoes to chew!" ❼

Stop and Think

❼ Why does April offer to share Buttons with Mrs. Ramirez?

April offers to share Buttons with her because _____

_____

_____

Think Critically

1. What does April realize about Buttons? PLOT

April realizes that Buttons _____

_____

_____

2. What can you tell about Mrs. Ramirez? Copy the web, and fill it in. CHARACTER

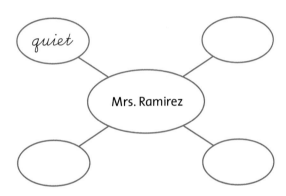

3. How do you think the author feels about owning pets? AUTHOR'S PURPOSE

I think the author feels that _____

_____

_____

_____

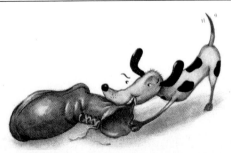

excursions
giddy
gleeful
panic
pinnacle
precious
turbulent

Vocabulary

Build Robust Vocabulary

Write the Vocabulary Word that completes each sentence. The first one has been done for you.

Gus the grasshopper was not happy. If Carmine would have let him out of his cage, he would have felt

(1) _____gleeful_____ . He looked out the window at the trees. A **(2)** _____ wind was causing them to sway back and forth. Gus wished he could feel that wind, too.

Gus longed for freedom. He wanted to go on exciting

(3) _____ like other grasshoppers. But he was locked in this cage. Gus knew that Carmine would never let him go. Gus was **(4)** _____ to the boy.

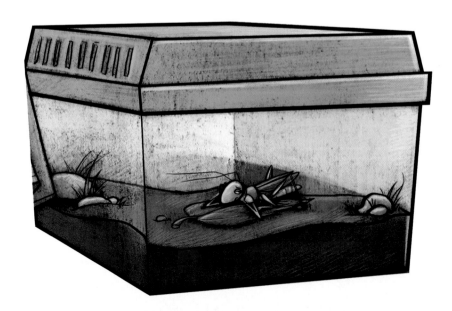

Gus went to sleep thinking about all this. Soon,

he was being nudged awake. He felt fear and

(5) _____ when he saw a strange

grasshopper in his cage.

Greta said she was there to save him. Gus was

(6) _____ with joy. He felt so silly

he could have danced. He followed Greta outside.

They climbed to the **(7)** _____

of a tree branch. What adventures

were ahead?

Write the answers to these questions. Use complete sentences.

8. What might someone do if he or she feels panic?

_____

_____

9. What kind of excursions do you think grasshoppers have?

_____

_____

CARMINE'S BACKYARD

by Jane Simon • illustrated by Dani Jones

Gus crouched in his cage in the kitchen. For a grasshopper, he was quite handsome, except when he scowled.

"Here I am in this dumb cage," Gus muttered to himself. "And I am bored, bored, bored. I never get to go on any excursions! All I do is sit here and watch the wind blow."

He stared at the limbs of the trees as they twisted in the turbulent wind.

"Time for lunch!" a cheerful voice called.

It was Carmine, his caretaker. Carmine unlocked the cage door and tossed in some grass and leaves. ❶

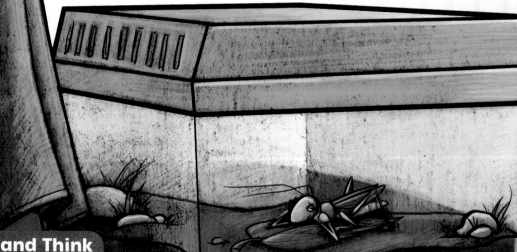

Stop and Think

❶ How can you tell that this story is a fantasy?

I can tell this is a fantasy because _____

_____

_____

© Harcourt

Gus just ignored the food. At first, Carmine was baffled, and then he was annoyed. "Wow, Gus, you look so miserable. What's the matter? Honestly, I give you tasty treats and keep your cage tidy. You even get to look out the kitchen window. I doubt any grasshopper has a better life than yours!"

Gus didn't twitch. Carmine frowned and started to fasten the lock on the cage door. Suddenly the phone rang and he hastened off.

Gus hid under a leaf, more miserable than ever. "Ha! I doubt I'm going to feel cheery any time soon," he grumbled. He combed the bristles on his green legs. Then he fell asleep. ❷

Stop and Think

❷ What do you know about Gus so far?

I know that _____

_____

_____

The next thing Gus knew, a dainty foot was nudging him. "Gus!" an excited voice whispered. "Wake up! I've been trying to wake you for about an hour!"

Gus felt panic. *How did this strange grasshopper get into his cage?* he wondered. *Carmine always fastened the lock!*

This grasshopper seemed to read his mind. "Today's your lucky day!" she exclaimed. "Carmine forgot to fasten the cage door. We mustn't waste time, so let's go!"

"But I haven't been outside this cage since I was a young lad!" Gus replied, suddenly scared. "I doubt I'm brave enough to go." ❸

Stop and Think

❸ Why was the other grasshopper able to get into the cage?

She was able to get into the cage because _____

_____

_____

"Nonsense!" said the grasshopper. "Just follow me."
She scrambled off the windowsill. Just then, Gus heard
Carmine's footsteps. He was coming into the kitchen again!
He must decide. It was now or never!

He lunged off the windowsill and landed with a
thud on the ground. Just like that, he was free! This new
independence made him giddy. He felt so dizzy that he
staggered into the coiled shape of a garden hose. It seemed
as big as a castle to Gus. **4**

Stop and Think

4 Why does the garden hose seem as big as a castle?

It seems as big as a castle because _____

_____

_____

Gus scurried to keep up with his new friend. They climbed over stones and passed a column of ants, marching in step. At last, they bounded under a bush where it was safe to stop.

"I'm forever in your debt for my precious freedom, but I don't even know you," Gus gasped, out of breath.

"My name is Greta, and I've got a surprise for you, Gus. Listen!" A weak rhythm floated across the lawn. Sometimes it echoed loudly. Then it seemed to soften. *Whatever could it be?* Gus wondered. **5**

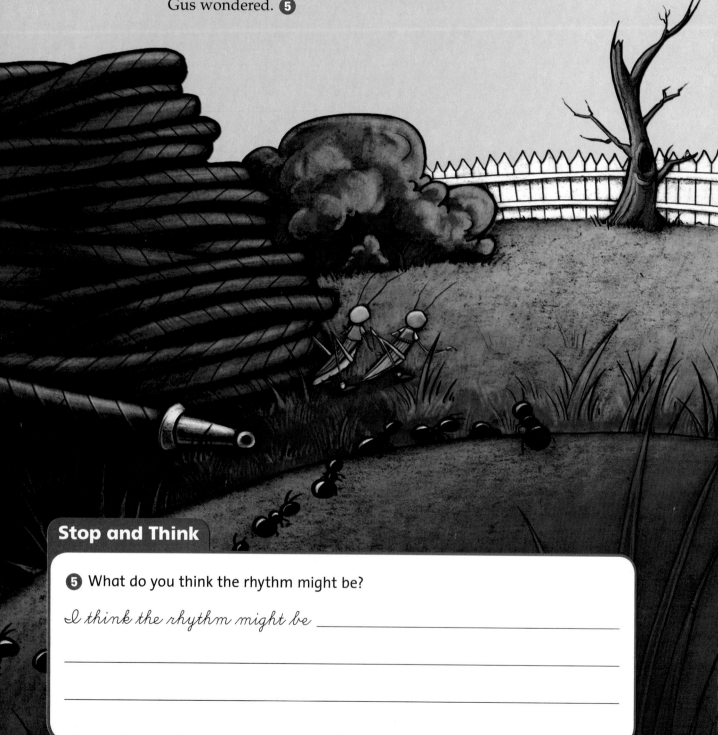

Stop and Think

5 What do you think the rhythm might be?

I think the rhythm might be _____

_____

_____

Greta led Gus to the far end of the backyard. The rhythm got even louder as they hopped along. Greta climbed up the trunk of a tree and along a large, dead limb that jutted into the air. She scurried to the very top. Then, in a flash, she disappeared!

"Now what?" Gus exclaimed. At last, he took a deep breath and decided to follow. He climbed up and up, to the very pinnacle of the limb. There he found an opening, a doorway really, into the tree. He could still hear the rhythm from down below. Gus climbed into the opening. **6**

Stop and Think

6 What do you think Gus will find inside the tree?

I think that Gus will find _____

_____

_____

Gus hopped down a dark tunnel and into a large hall. The room was filled with gleeful grasshoppers. They whistled and cheered when they saw him.

"Please join us, Gus, in a chant to your freedom," declared an old brown grasshopper.

"Hear, hear!" responded a thousand more grasshoppers, and they began to chirp loudly. Their chirping rhythm swirled through the air.

Gus smiled at Greta, and began to chirp, too. He had come home, and he'd never been more content, or less bored, in his entire grasshopper life. **7**

Stop and Think

7 Why is Gus content now?

Gus is content now because _____

_____

_____

Think Critically

1. What happens in the story? Copy the story map, and fill it in. PLOT

Characters	Setting

Plot Events

1. *Gus is bored and lonely in his cage.*

2.

3.

4.

2. Why is Gus afraid to follow Greta? CHARACTER

Gus is afraid because _____

_____

_____

3. How do you think the author feels about Gus? AUTHOR'S PURPOSE

I think the author feels _____

_____

_____

Vocabulary

Build Robust Vocabulary

Write the word that best completes each sentence.
The first one has been done for you.

1. Volunteers like to help others. They show

_____altruism_____ in their communities in

coordination   panic   altruism

several ways.

2. Some volunteers fix up _____ houses to

dilapidated   bland   turbulent

make them nice and safe again.

3. An adult _____ can teach volunteers

damage   mentor   pinnacle

how to do a good job.

4. Some volunteers take care of animals that have been hurt

and _____ .

immaculate   mistreated   dilapidated

5. One volunteer said he used to _____

detect   bustle   loathe

reading aloud, but now he likes it. He's helping people who
can't see well enough to read.

© Harcourt

6. When reading, the volunteer uses his artistic

_____ to add drama to the story.

damage   sensibility   altruism

7. Some volunteers bake tasty treats—not

_____ ones—to raise money for

precious   gleeful   bland

community projects.

8. One volunteer started a new _____

advocacy   sensibility   cumbersome

group to help protect law-enforcement dogs.

9. It takes a lot of _____ to complete some

coordination   mentor   panic

projects; volunteers must work together.

10. If you are _____ and caring, you too can

compassionate   deflated   desolate

become a community volunteer.

Write the answers to these questions. Use complete sentences.

11. Why would someone want a mentor? _____

_____

12. What could you do to improve bland food? _____

_____

KID POWER!

by Jeff Putnam • illustrated by Frank Morrison

CHARACTERS

Blake Robins	Dana Bowman	Morgan Cook
Luis Ramirez	Anna Lopez	Bailey Foster
Mitch Wu	Payton March	

Blake Robins: Good afternoon, everyone. You're tuned to Kid Power on the Air. I'm Blake Robins.

Luis Ramirez: I'm Luis Ramirez, and today's show is about kids making a difference. How do they make a difference? By working as volunteers!

Blake Robins: That's right, Luis. Some kids are fixing up dilapidated houses, while others are taking care of mistreated pets. First, listen to how one girl has put her gift for baking to excellent use. Let's go to Mitch Wu. **1**

Stop and Think

1 What do you think you will learn about in this selection?

I think I will learn about _____

_____

_____

© Harcourt

Mitch Wu: Thanks, guys. I'm here with Dana Bowman. Dana, tell us about your job.

Dana Bowman: Well, Mitch, I just enjoy baking. You ought to try some of my awesome banana bread.

Mitch Wu: But I thought Kid Power projects helped communities.

Dana Bowman: That's correct, Mitch. My pals and I felt the town ought to put a bike path through our neighborhoods. We started a weekly bake sale to raise funds for the path.

Mitch Wu: So, is the project going well? **2**

Stop and Think

2 How does Dana put her talent to good use?

Dana puts her talent to good use by _____

_____

_____

Dana Bowman: Yes, it's been a fantastic way to get things rolling, so to speak. Oh, excuse me, Mitch, I ought to get back and add some fruit to my dough—I don't want it to turn out too bland! Our customers like the sweet treats best.

Mitch Wu: Good luck, Dana, and now back to Luis and Blake.

Luis Ramirez: Thanks, Mitch. Our next Kid Power story is from reporter Anna Lopez.

Anna Lopez: Meet Bailey Foster, a compassionate kid who has a soft spot for dogs. Tell us about your project, Bailey. ❸

Stop and Think

❸ What are two meanings of Dana's phrase "get things rolling"?

Two meanings of this phrase are _____

_____

_____

© Harcourt

Bailey Foster: I read that some law-enforcement dogs get injured on the job. I didn't like the thought of any dogs getting hurt, so I started an advocacy group to raise money to buy safety vests. We perform small jobs throughout the neighborhood to raise the money.

Anna Lopez: How many vests do you plan to purchase?

Bailey Foster: Well, our goal is for every dog throughout the state to have a vest.

Anna Lopez: Wow—that's a lot. Have you asked for help? **4**

Stop and Think

4 Do you think safety vests for police dogs are a good idea? Explain.

I think that safety vests are _____

_____

_____

© Harcourt

Bailey Foster: Yes, we asked our state senator to help us. I consider her my mentor since she's teaching me how to start large projects like this one.

Anna Lopez: A project like this must take a lot of coordination.

Bailey Foster: Yes, it's tough, but we all work together.

Anna Lopez: Thanks for talking to us, Bailey.

Luis Ramirez: We'll look next at a compassionate girl who has turned her talent for words into a worthy project. Morgan Cook has the story. ❺

Stop and Think

❺ What can you tell about Bailey?

I can tell that Bailey _____

_____

_____

© Harcourt

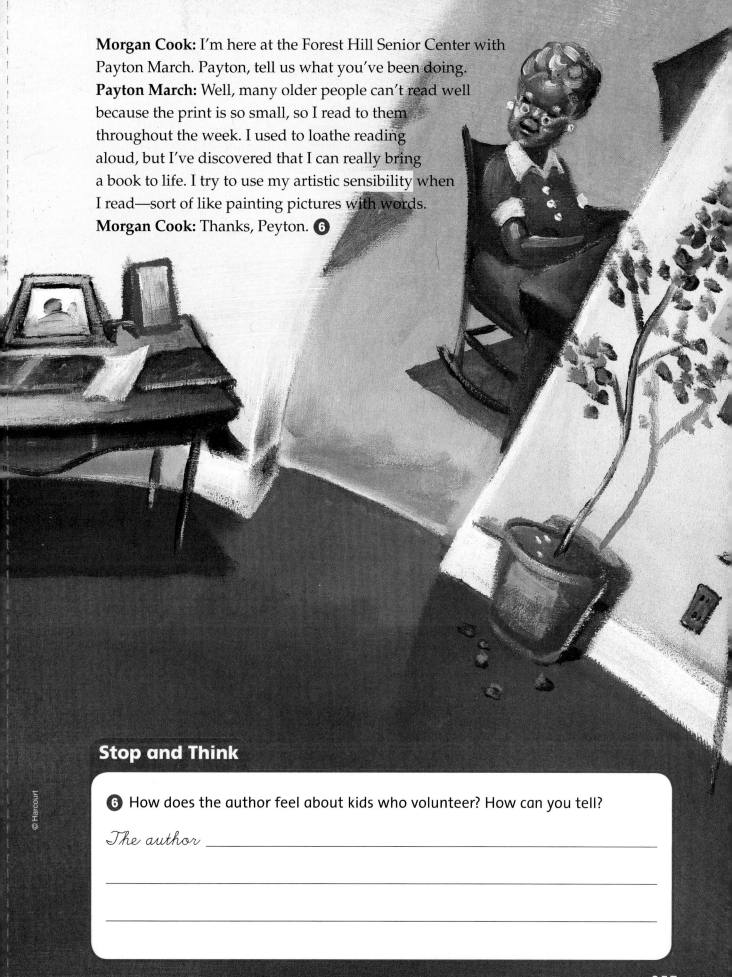

Morgan Cook: I'm here at the Forest Hill Senior Center with Payton March. Payton, tell us what you've been doing.

Payton March: Well, many older people can't read well because the print is so small, so I read to them throughout the week. I used to loathe reading aloud, but I've discovered that I can really bring a book to life. I try to use my artistic sensibility when I read—sort of like painting pictures with words.

Morgan Cook: Thanks, Peyton. **6**

Stop and Think

6 How does the author feel about kids who volunteer? How can you tell?

The author _____

_____

_____

Blake Robins: Great job, Morgan, and let's say a big thanks to all of our reporters. They've shown us that, throughout the community, kids are making a difference in so many ways.

Luis Ramirez: That's right, Blake. And we've also discovered that altruism can be shown to both people *and* animals.

Blake Robins: We'll leave you with some food for thought: How are *you* making a difference in your community? **7**

Stop and Think

7 How could you use your own talents to help others?

I could _____

_____

_____

© Harcourt

Think Critically

1. What examples does the author use to support the main idea of kids helping others? MAIN IDEA AND DETAILS

   The author uses the examples of _____

   _____

   _____

   _____

2. What traits do all of the volunteers have in common? CHARACTERS

   The volunteers are all _____

   _____

   _____

   _____

3. How does this selection make you feel about volunteering? AUTHOR'S PURPOSE

   This selection makes me feel _____

   _____

   _____

   _____

asset

dismal

esteem

intently

ordeal

peril

profusely

terrain

Vocabulary

Build Robust Vocabulary

Read the selection and think about the meanings of the words in dark type.

On April 9, 1922, Charles Lindbergh took to the skies for the first time. After working as a pilot, Lindbergh later discovered a contest that would change his life.

A New York man was offering a prize of $25,000 to the first person to fly non-stop across the Atlantic alone. Pilots everywhere talked **profusely** about this contest. Many pilots believed that it could not be done. Lindbergh would **esteem** it to be an adventure that was worth the risk.

Lindbergh decided to try the flight across the Atlantic. He refitted his plane for the **ordeal,** since it needed to be light to travel 3,600 miles. Every ounce mattered, so Lindbergh took out a leather seat and a gas tank dial. He even trimmed his paper maps that would help him identify the **terrain** below during his flight. One change added to Lindbergh's **peril.** He took out one of the two engines, leaving the plane with just a single engine.

On the morning of May 20, 1927, Lindbergh set out on his trans-Atlantic flight. Soon after sunset, he ran into **dismal** weather. Lindbergh's bravery was an **asset.** He gazed into the night **intently** as he flew on through fog, ice, and sleet into unknown skies.

Write the answers to these questions. Use complete sentences.
The first one has been done for you.

1. What does it mean when someone talks **profusely** about something?
It means they talked about something a lot because it was interesting.

2. What kind of man do you **esteem** Lindbergh to be?

_____

_____

3. If Lindbergh's trans-Atlantic flight was an **ordeal,** what was it like?

_____

_____

4. How can a map help a pilot identify **terrain**?

_____

_____

5. Why do you think **dismal** weather adds to a pilot's **peril**?

_____

_____

6. What are three **assets** that you think would have been necessary
for Lindbergh to make the flight?

_____

_____

7. What was Lindbergh doing when he gazed **intently** ahead?

_____

_____

Charles Lindbergh,
the Lone Eagle

by Jeff Putnam
illustrated by Paul Tong

The little airplane was alone over the dark sea, with almost no stars shining in the sky. The plane flew through thick haze and around huge clouds as the pilot gazed intently into the night. He later recalled, "There was no moon, and it was very dark."

The year was 1927, and the pilot was Charles Lindbergh, a 25-year-old man from Minnesota. In front of him lay 3,000 miles of unknown sea. Lindbergh's goal was France. He was trying to do something no one had ever accomplished before: fly solo across the Atlantic. **1**

Stop and Think

1 What do you learn about Charles Lindbergh?

I learn that Charles Lindbergh _____

_____

_____

Charles Lindbergh grew up on his family's farm in Minnesota. One day, he looked up into the sky and saw an airplane flying overhead. How did Charles react to this astonishing sight? From that moment on, he was itching to fly.

On April 9, 1922, Lindbergh took to the skies for the first time. The experience sparked a lifelong pursuit of flight. He worked at several airplane jobs just so he could satisfy his need to fly. Most of these jobs were unsafe and involved stunt flying, or performing daring tricks in mid-air. Lindbergh danced with disaster every time he was in the air, making spectators on the ground uneasy. Luckily, he escaped from several crashes unharmed. **2**

Stop and Think

2 What does it mean to be "itching to fly"?

It means that _____

_____

_____

After he bought his first plane in 1923, Lindbergh worked as an air mail pilot, flying mail between Chicago and St. Louis five times a week. Then he discovered a contest that would change his life.

A New York man was offering a prize of $25,000 to the first person to fly non-stop across the Atlantic alone. Many flyers tried the challenging feat, but they all failed. Lindbergh convinced some people to help him win the prize. These rich backers gave him money to buy a plane and equipment for the trip. At the same time, five other challengers were attempting the crossing—and Lindbergh wanted to be first. **3**

Stop and Think

3 How would you describe Charles Lindbergh?

Charles Lindbergh _____

_____

_____

Lindbergh named his plane *The Spirit of St. Louis*. He would later esteem it a "wonderful plane . . . like a living creature, gliding along smoothly."

Lindbergh refitted a plane for the ordeal, since it needed to be light to travel 3,600 miles. Every ounce mattered, so Lindbergh took out a leather seat, a gas tank dial, and all heavy things. He even trimmed his paper maps and wore extra-light boots!

This uncommon plane had very long wings, and its gas tanks were reshaped to be larger than normal so they would hold more gas. But another necessary change, while lightening the weight, added to Lindbergh's peril. Lindbergh took out one of the two engines, leaving the plane with just a single engine. If that engine failed, the plane would disappear into the Atlantic. **4**

Stop and Think

4 How did Lindbergh refit his plane?

Lindbergh refitted his plane by _____

_____

_____

On the morning of May 20, 1927, *The Spirit of St. Louis* took off from a New York airport, with Lindbergh in the pilot's seat. The time was 7:52 P.M., and a crowd of more than five hundred people gathered to wish him good luck.

Soon after sunset, Lindbergh ran into dismal weather when ice coated the plane's wings and thick fog blanketed all the windows. At times, he was only 10 feet above the white-capping waves of the Atlantic. As the hours dragged on, Lindbergh grew weary, but never discouraged. He knew he couldn't sleep; his life depended on staying awake. His resolve was an unmatched asset. **5**

Stop and Think

5 Do you think Lindbergh will make it across the Atlantic? Explain.

I think that Lindbergh _____

_____

_____

Lindbergh's route across the Atlantic

Then, after more than thirty hours in the air, he spied a fishing boat floating below him in the water. Seeing a boat meant that he was close to land. Lindbergh rechecked his maps and the terrain below, and found he was off the coast of Ireland. With a spark of newfound energy, he redirected his plane south—for France!

Soon, day faded again into night, and still Lindbergh flew on, looking for Paris. Then Lindbergh saw the lights of a landing strip ahead, along with the unexpected lights of hundreds of cars! Every road leading to the airport was jammed with cars. People sat on car hoods or milled around, waiting to greet the hero Lindbergh. **6**

Stop and Think

6 How do you think Lindbergh felt when he saw the cars? Why?

I think he felt _____

_____

_____

An instant after Lindbergh landed, the crowd rushed at the plane, cheering profusely and shouting "Lindbergh! Lindbergh!" The excitement was unreal and Lindbergh was unable to move in the crush, so men had to lift him over the crowd. The unknown pilot from Minnesota had claimed the $25,000 prize—as well as a place in history.

Back in the United States, people were so proud of his solitary flight that they gave him a nickname—the Lone Eagle. The boy who once dreamed of flying was now on top of the world! **7**

Stop and Think

7 Why was Lindbergh called the "Lone Eagle"?

He was called the "Lone Eagle" because _____

_____

_____

Think Critically

1. How did Lindbergh become known as the Lone Eagle? Copy the chart, and fill in the two columns. **SUMMARIZE AND PARAPHRASE**

Ideas	Summary	Paraphrase
• Refitted a plane. • Flew across the Atlantic alone. • Called the Lone Eagle.		

2. How do you think the author feels about Charles Lindbergh? **AUTHOR'S VIEWPOINT**

I think the author feels _____

_____

_____

3. How did Lindbergh make his flight a successful one? **MAIN IDEA AND DETAILS**

Lindbergh _____

_____

_____

© Harcourt

269

appalled

floundered

grueling

invest

isolated

laden

remote

Vocabulary

Build Robust Vocabulary

Write the Vocabulary Word that completes each sentence in the newspaper articles. The first one has been done for you.

DAILY NEWS   SECTION C

DAILY N[...]

Peary and Henson Return from North Pole!

by Lee Johnson   August 17, 1909

Explorers Robert Peary and Matthew Henson have returned from their trip to the North Pole! The North Pole was extremely difficult to reach. It's certainly the most

(1) _____isolated_____ place in the world.

It was a **(2)** _____ trip that demanded a lot from the team. But these brave explorers managed to reach this **(3)** _____ area that is so far away from any settlement. We are sure Peary and Henson had no idea they would have to **(4)** _____ eighteen years in this project. But their success no doubt makes it all worthwhile.

Henson and Peary Give Details

by Lee Johnson   August 20, 1909

Matthew Henson and Robert Peary are back from their trip to the North Pole. They began their trip in February of this year. Henson said they traveled with six dog-team sledges that were **(5)** _____ with food and supplies.

Then the explorers told of the most dangerous part of their trip. Some men were asleep in two igloos they had made on the ice. The ice began to break up, and one igloo started to float away. Men and dogs **(6)** _____ in the icy cold, trying to escape. In the end, they were able to get to a safe spot. The explorers were **(7)** _____ at the speed with which the ice broke up.

After that, the trip became a little easier, despite the bitter cold. At last, on April 6, 1909, Peary determined that they had reached the North Pole.

To the Arctic

with Matthew Henson

by Margie Sigman ✳ map illustrated by Bill Reynolds

Matthew Henson's remarkable life began in Maryland, where he was born in 1866. His parents were very poor farmers. By the time Henson was thirteen, he went out to find work. He tried a few odd jobs, but he was restless and bored. The explorer in Henson dreamed about seeing new places and learning new things. Finally, he walked a day's hike to the seaport in Baltimore. There he was hired as a cabin boy on the ship *Katy Hines*.

During his years at sea, Henson saw nearly every continent. The kindly skipper of his ship taught him to read and write. After his sailing days ended, Henson returned to the east coast and worked at several different jobs, including one in a hat store. **1**

Stop and Think

1 What happened to Matthew Henson at sea?

At sea, Matthew Henson _____

_____

_____

One day, the explorer Robert Peary came into Henson's store. When Peary said he was looking for a suitable assistant, the store owner suggested Henson. Together, Henson and Peary would invest eighteen years of their lives trying to reach the North Pole.

On trips to the Arctic, Henson quickly made friends with the Inuit, the people who lived there. He even learned how to speak Inuit. Unlike some explorers, Henson was respectful of the Inuits' way of life. Most importantly, he showed them over and over that he was an honorable man. From the wise Inuit, Henson learned how to survive in the harsh Arctic. **2**

❄ **Robert Peary**

❄ **Matthew Henson with the Inuit**

Stop and Think

2 Why was it helpful for Henson to speak Inuit?

It was helpful because _____

_____

_____

The first five trips to the Arctic were grueling. On each attempt, Peary and Henson had to turn back before they reached the North Pole. Usually, bad luck or bad weather was the problem. Illness, broken equipment, or injury could delay them as often as a heavy storm. As beautiful as the Arctic can be, it is a remote and deadly place.

In the Arctic, Henson was a valuable person to have around. He was one of the best dog handlers and drivers in the North. When supplies were low, he hunted for food. He skillfully cut blocks of snow and ice to make igloos. Henson knew how to dress warmly for survival and how to repair a sledge. **3**

❄ The team prepared the dogs for the trip.

Stop and Think

3 Why would Henson be a good person to have with you in the Arctic?

Having Henson would be good because _____

_____

_____

In February, 1909, Peary and Henson began their sixth attempt to reach the North Pole. Their six dog-team sledges were heavily laden with food and supplies. The trail stretched all the way across the frozen water of the Arctic Ocean. The temperature was well below freezing—a killing cold. Boots froze to men's feet, and even breathing could be painful.

Leaving land, the explorers struggled over the choppy ice. Some chunks were high above their heads. Even the tireless sled dogs became exhausted. When a sledge finally broke on the rough ice, Henson repaired it. He threaded line through new holes in the sled with his bare hands. **4**

❄ **Men and dogs struggled over the rough ice.**

Stop and Think

4 What does the author mean when she says it was "a killing cold"?

She means that _____

_____

_____

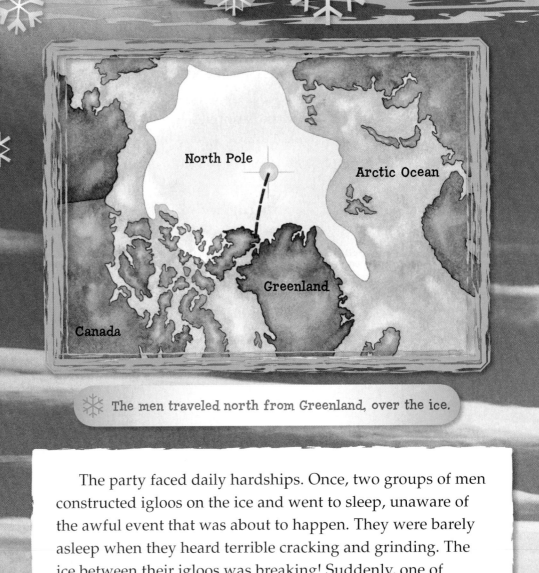

The men traveled north from Greenland, over the ice.

The party faced daily hardships. Once, two groups of men constructed igloos on the ice and went to sleep, unaware of the awful event that was about to happen. They were barely asleep when they heard terrible cracking and grinding. The ice between their igloos was breaking! Suddenly, one of the igloos began to float away. Men and dogs floundered in the bitter cold, then scrambled across the ice and water to safety. Henson was appalled at how quickly everything had fallen apart. But amazingly, no one drowned. **5**

Stop and Think

5 What awful event occurred one time on the ice?

One time, _____

_____

_____

They left a flag where land ended and ice began.

Finally, the team made their last camp in the isolated North. From here, only Peary, Henson, and four Inuit men would make the final journey to the North Pole.

The weather was surprisingly agreeable on this last part of the trip. The dogs trotted easily in their harnesses, and the handful of men traveled smoothly over the mostly flat ice. Never before had anyone gotten this close to the North Pole.

On April 6, 1909, Commander Peary called a halt and peered at the flat, empty expanse of ice around them. Had they reached their goal? Since the North Pole is simply an imaginary point on the Arctic Ocean, there were no landmarks. **6**

Stop and Think

6 What do you think Peary will do next?

I think Peary will _____

_____

_____

Peary needed to take several readings of the sun at different times to find out exactly where they were. He sighted, measured, and carefully noted the numbers as Henson and the other men waited excitedly. Finally, the commander announced the results. They had reached the North Pole!

Henson could hardly believe it. His years of exploring had led him here, to this beautiful place at the very top of the earth.

After a life of accomplishment, Henson died in 1955. On his gravestone, his own words sum up this eventful life: "The lure of the Arctic is tugging at my heart. To me the trail is calling. The old trail. The trail that is always new." **7**

The team, with Henson in the middle, hefted flags at the Pole.

Stop and Think

7 Why do the words on Henson's gravestone sum up his life?

They sum up his life because _____

_____

_____

Think Critically

1. What do you learn about Henson's eventful life? Copy the chart, and fill it in. **SUMMARIZE AND PARAPHRASE**

Ideas	Summary	Paraphrase
• Born in 1866. • Tried many jobs. • Explored the Arctic for eighteen years. • Learned how to survive from the Inuit. • Reached the North Pole on April 6, 1909.		

2. How did Henson help to make the trip successful? **MAIN IDEA AND DETAILS**

Henson helped by _____

_____

_____

3. What made Henson a good Arctic explorer? **CHARACTER**

Henson was a good Arctic explorer because _____

_____

_____

Vocabulary

Build Robust Vocabulary

Write the Vocabulary Word that completes each sentence. The first one has been done for you.

Earth is surrounded by a blanket of air called the *atmosphere.* The lowest layer, about 7.5 miles thick, is higher than the **(1)** _____**summit**_____ of the tallest mountain. This layer contains 90 percent of our planet's air. All of our weather changes take place here.

Without help, no one can live beyond this lower layer of atmosphere. But some men and women do go beyond it—into space. They are taken there by rockets with **(2)** _____ designs. A great deal of force is needed to lift heavy rockets beyond the atmosphere and into space.

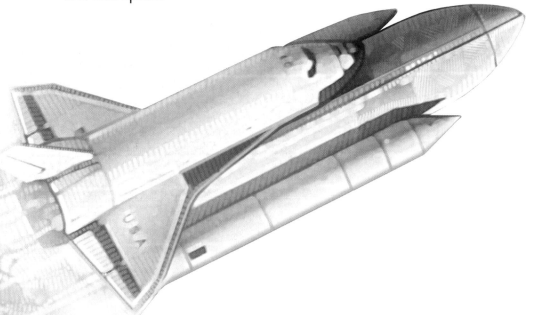

Astronauts go to the International Space Station (ISS) 220 miles above Earth. They must quickly get **(3)** _____ to life there. Astronauts study many things in space. One thing they want to know is how plants, animals, and humans **(4)** _____ to life without gravity.

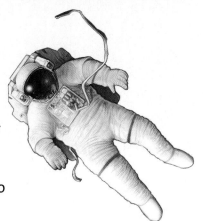

To keep muscles strong, it is **(5)** _____ to exercise while in space. Sleeping bags must be hooked to a wall to stay **(6)** _____ . Imagine trying to sleep if your bag kept drifting through the cabin, bumping into things!

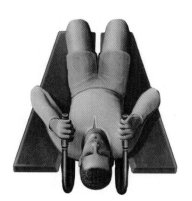

Write the Vocabulary Word that best completes the synonym web.

7.

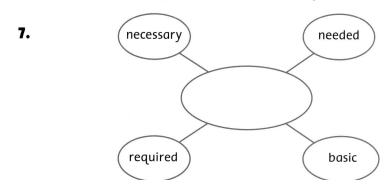

necessary

needed

required

basic

Life in Space

by Jeff Putnam • illustrated by Eric Williams

Have you ever thought about making your home in space? Some people do live in space. Someday, you could, too.

Home, Sweet Home

Our home is a huge globe surrounded by endless space. We call it Earth. A blanket of air called the *atmosphere* surrounds Earth. The atmosphere allows us to breathe and protects us from the extreme heat of the sun. During the night, it protects us from the terrible cold of space. The lowest layer, higher than the summit of the tallest mountain in the world, is about 7.5 miles (12 kilometers) thick. This layer contains 90 percent of Earth's air, as well as its weather. It's impossible to live beyond this lowest layer—without help. **1**

Stop and Think

1 What do you want to know about life in space?

I want to know _____

_____

_____

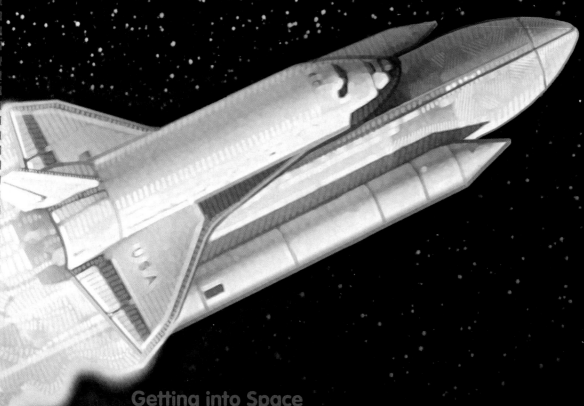

Getting into Space

The first hurdle to jump is just getting into space! Powerful, streamlined rockets carry people into space. They burn fuel and produce hot gases, which boost them into space.

Sometimes, the rocket carries a smaller craft called a shuttle. Shuttles make more than one trip; rockets don't. The shuttle separates from the rocket, and the rocket's parts fall back to Earth. Then the shuttle, with trained astronauts aboard, continues its trip into space.

Next stop—the International Space Station (ISS), a laboratory in space! **2**

Stop and Think

2 What do you think you will learn about next?

I think I will learn about _____

_____

_____

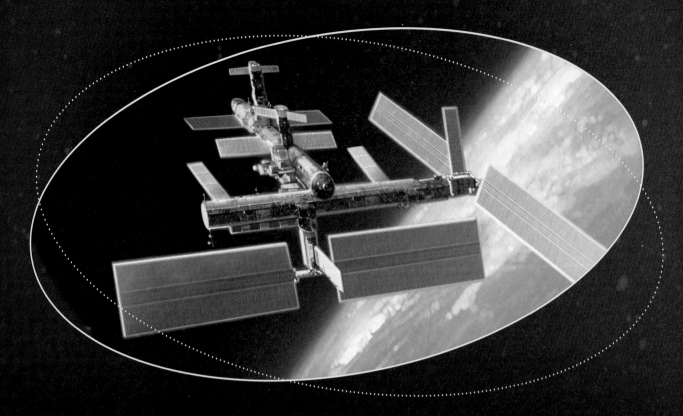

Wait For Me!

The ISS is really moving! To catch it, be ready to match its speed of 17,000 miles (27,350 kilometers) per hour. It's way up there, too—220 miles (352 kilometers) above Earth. But you finally reach it and dock. Climb through the hatches, and you're ready to settle down in space.

Your New Home

Your new home in space is enormous. The ISS is almost as long as a football field and weighs about a million pounds (453,592 kilograms). Engineers from around the world put it together over several years. The different pieces were constructed on Earth, then flown up and pieced together in space. ❸

Stop and Think

❸ How does the author make you feel about traveling in space?

The author makes me feel _____

_____

_____

How Is Space Different from Earth?

For one thing, you're weightless in space. There's no gravity, so you float around the cabin. The problem is, so does everything else! You have to avoid bumping into other astronauts and strap down both your food and nonfood items. Drinking without a straw is very impractical in space. And don't even try taking a shower—it's impossible!

Daily Life in Space

Astronauts living in space do lots of tests. Before take-off, they prepare experiments. Once in space, they study plants to see how they grow. They raise mice, chicks, spiders, frogs, and other nonhuman passengers to see how they acclimate to life without gravity. ④

Stop and Think

④ Which words on this page contain prefixes meaning "not," "no," or "the opposite of"? Underline them.

Words that contain these prefixes are _____

_____

Living in space requires lots of equipment. Here's a preview of some of the things you might need.

Sleeping bag – It hooks to a wall so you're secure and immobile.

Space toys – During nonwork times, astronauts play with balls, jacks, marbles, and even a yo-yo.

Space music – Jamming in space is cool! But it's impolite to play when anyone is trying to sleep.

Slippers – Maybe you already have a pair just like these. Bring them along! **5**

Stop and Think

5 Why do you think living in space requires lots of equipment?

I think it requires lots of equipment because _____

_____

_____

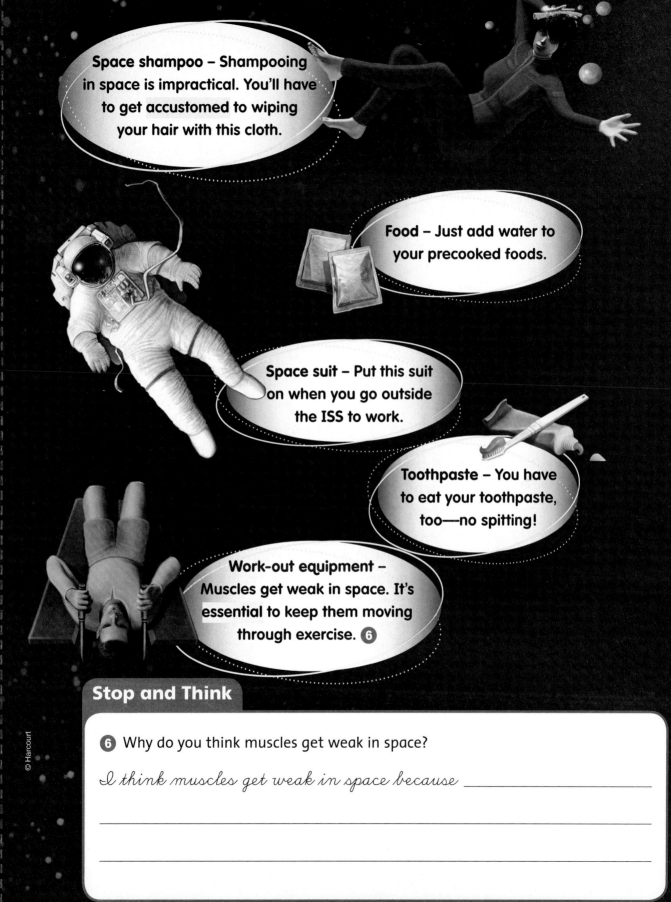

Space shampoo – Shampooing in space is impractical. You'll have to get accustomed to wiping your hair with this cloth.

Food – Just add water to your precooked foods.

Space suit – Put this suit on when you go outside the ISS to work.

Toothpaste – You have to eat your toothpaste, too—no spitting!

Work-out equipment – Muscles get weak in space. It's essential to keep them moving through exercise. 6

Stop and Think

6 Why do you think muscles get weak in space?

I think muscles get weak in space because _____

_____

_____

© Harcourt

The Future in Space

What is the future of life in space? Can you picture a hotel in space? Don't dismiss it as nonsense. How about a space wedding? Can you picture a mine on the moon or on Mars? Maybe a fish farm? These ideas aren't impossible. They may seem improbable, but each could happen in the future. Today's space researchers are working nonstop to come up with new ideas for life in space. Maybe you'll be the one to test out their ideas. Oh, and don't forget your slippers! ❼

Stop and Think

❼ Are the author's statements about future life in space facts or opinions? Explain your answer.

The statements about future life in space are _____

_____

_____

Think Critically

1. What have you learned about life in space? Copy the chart, and fill in the third column. **MAIN IDEA AND DETAILS**

K	W	L

2. How is life in the space station different from life on Earth? **COMPARE AND CONTRAST**

Here is how life in the space station is different:

_____

_____

_____

3. Do you think you would like to live in space? Explain. **PERSONAL RESPONSE**

I think that _____

_____

_____

Vocabulary

Build Robust Vocabulary

Write the Vocabulary Word that completes each sentence in the selection. The first one has been done for you.

In 1768, Captain James Cook led a mission from England to Tahiti. His job was to see how long it took the planet Venus to pass in front of the Sun. This information would **(1)** _____ potentially _____ help researchers figure out the distance from the Sun to Earth.

With ninety-five crew members and all their supplies, Cook's ship was very **(2)** _____ when it set out from England. Because the ship was made of wood, crew members had to be very careful with fire. The ship could be **(3)** _____ if any crew member was careless.

Cook and his crew were glad to get to Tahiti. The

(4) _____ of the island was a peaceful relief

after months at sea.

Cook began observing Venus on June 3, 1769. He was

(5) _____ into a telescope, trying to time

Venus's trip across the Sun. But the outline of Venus was too

fuzzy. It was hard to tell exactly when the planet's trip across the

Sun began and ended. There was a great deal of confusion. In the

end, the whole project had to be scrapped.

Cook continued exploring the South Pacific. He wanted to

make accurate maps of the area. At one point, he collided with the

Great Barrier Reef. The ship took on water, and all heavy objects had

to be **(6)** _____ so the ship wouldn't sink. You

will read more about Cook's adventures in "To the South Pacific."

TO THE
SOUTH
PACIFIC

by Linda Barr • illustrated by Cathy Morrison

Every 120 years, the planet Venus passes in front of the Sun. This event is called the Transit of Venus. It can be seen from only a few places on Earth.

In 1768, researchers in England were preparing for the Transit of Venus in 1769. They wanted to send out people to observe the Transit from different places. One of these places was Tahiti in the South Pacific. But they were unclear about its exact location.

The researchers hoped to use the Transit of Venus to figure out the distance from the Sun to Earth. They planned to find out how far the remaining planets were from the Sun. **1**

Stop and Think

1 Why is observing the Transit of Venus important?

It's important because _____

_____

_____

The South Pacific was a tricky place to navigate. In 1768, there were few maps of the South Seas. Some mapmakers thought there was a giant continent in this area. Others didn't agree.

Tahiti is only twenty miles wide, a tiny speck in the vast seas. To reach it, a ship would have to cross thousands of miles of open water. Potentially, the ship could miss Tahiti completely.

The researchers asked James Cook, an experienced ship captain, to lead the dangerous mission. Cook's ship would sail alone and have no communication with England. It would have no protection from storms. If a fire ignited on board, the wooden ship would go up in flames. ❷

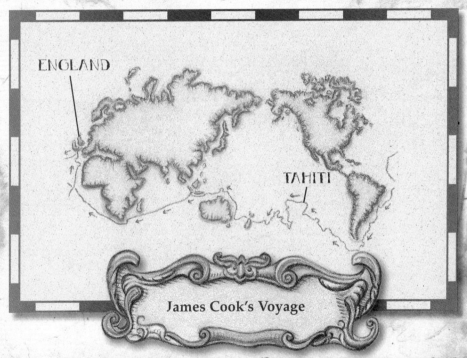

ENGLAND

TAHITI

James Cook's Voyage

Stop and Think

❷ Is the mission really dangerous? Explain.

The mission _____

_____

_____

On August 12, 1768, Cook's ship set sail with ninety-five crew members aboard. The cramped ship was filled with as many supplies as it could hold. The crew wouldn't be able to get any more food or water during the long trip across the seas.

From England, the ship sailed in a westerly direction and crossed the Atlantic. As it rounded the tip of South America, five men died in a storm. The ship sailed for ten more weeks across the South Pacific. The crew's food supply slowly disappeared. They had to catch fish to avoid starvation. **3**

Stop and Think

3 What do you want to know about Cook's mission?

I want to know _____

_____

_____

After eight long months, the ship finally reached Tahiti. The location was truly beautiful, causing much celebration among the crew. Tahiti was a vision of peace and tranquility. It almost took Cook's attention away from the reason for his trip—to witness the Transit of Venus!

Cook's instructions were to time how long this event took. On June 3, 1769, Cook finally made his observations of the Transit. Squinting into a telescope, he watched the motion of a small black disk as it slid across the Sun. But the outline of Venus was too fuzzy. It was hard to tell exactly when the planet's trip across the Sun began and ended. ❹

During the Transit, Venus looks like a tiny black dot sliding across the Sun.

Stop and Think

❹ What do you think will happen next?

I think that _____

_____

_____

Around the globe, other observers were also timing the Transit. Many of them recorded different times. This led to a great deal of confusion. It would be 120 more years before anyone could figure out the distances between the planets!

After Tahiti, Cook continued his explorations of the South Pacific, trying to find the legendary Great Southern Continent. It was thought to stretch across most of the southern Pacific and include what is now Australia. In time, Cook confirmed that the smaller continent of Australia was the only one in the South Pacific. Maps showing a giant continent in the South Pacific were now useless. **5**

Here, Cook observed the Transit of Venus.

Stop and Think

5 How did Cook's explorations affect mapmakers?

Cook's explorations caused _____

_____

_____

During one trip, Cook's ship had a collision with the Great Barrier Reef near what is now Australia. With the ship taking on water, all heavy objects were jettisoned overboard in order to lighten the load. Still, destruction to the ship forced Cook to land on the closest beach. Repairs took ten long weeks.

As Cook sailed, he drew maps of Earth's seas and coasts. With this new information, he made corrections on old maps. **6**

Stop and Think

6 Why does the author describe Cook's collision with the reef?

The author describes this because _____

_____

_____

Cook made several trips over the seas in his lifetime. His goal for two of those trips was to map the west coast of North America up to Alaska. At that time, there were many versions of maps of this coastline. Some were incomplete or even incorrect. In mapping this coast, Cook greatly reduced the confusion for others. His efforts made navigation safer there.

Before his death in 1779, Cook had mapped more than five thousand miles of coastline. Though his explorations were over, he had made such trips much easier and safer for future explorers. ➐

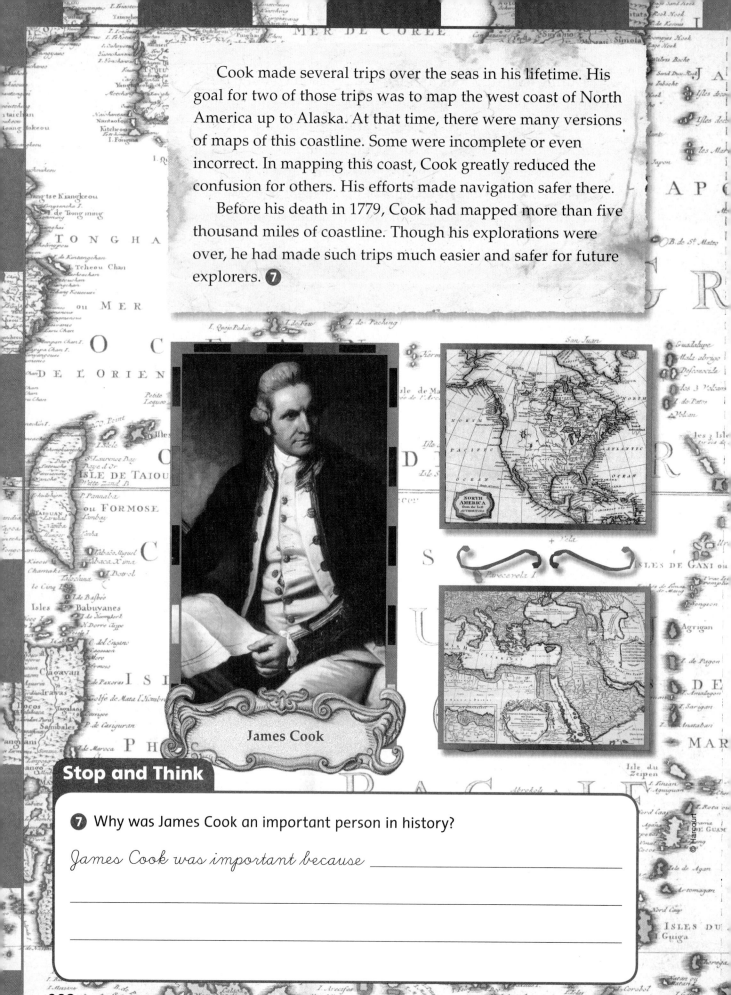

James Cook

Stop and Think

➐ Why was James Cook an important person in history?

James Cook was important because _____

_____

_____

~ Think Critically ~

1. What have you learned about James Cook's explorations? Copy the chart, and fill in the third column. MAIN IDEA AND DETAILS

K	W	L

2. How would you describe James Cook? CHARACTER

James Cook _____

_____

_____

3. Why are trips to the South Pacific easier and safer today?
CAUSE AND EFFECT

The trips are easier and safer because _____

_____

_____

Vocabulary

Build Robust Vocabulary

Write the word that best completes each sentence. The first one has been done for you.

1. If your understanding of caves is _____**insufficient**_____ ,

insufficient   regal   dismal

you should never explore a cave without an expert.

2. It's not only _____ , but also necessary

customary   exceptional   equivalent

to use the right equipment when exploring caves.

3. It's exciting when you're _____ at the

cramped   poised   regal

entrance of a cave, ready to go in.

4. Once inside, you may see _____ stone

remote   intent   exceptional

formations like no others you've seen before.

5. The special stone formations are called *stalactites*

and *stalagmites*. Some cave explorers speak

_____ about the need to protect them.

earnestly   potentially   customary

300

© Harcourt

6. Don't waste time _____ about how to

    provoking squinting bickering

explore a cave—just follow your leader.

7. Some stalagmites might be shaped like the

_____ throne of a king.

customary secure regal

8. You might see bats in a cave, but don't

_____ or scare them!

invest provoke isolate

9. A cave bat weighs the _____ of just four

    equivalent summit peril

wooden pencils.

10. If you successfully explore a cave, you can be proud of your

_____ .

equivalent achievement terrain

**Write the Vocabulary Word that best completes the
synonym web.**

11.

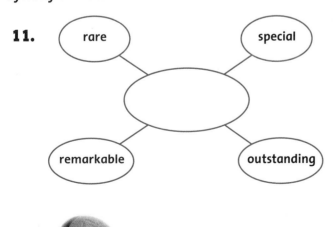

rare special remarkable outstanding

Exploring Caves

by Jeff Putnam • illustrated by Matthew Trueman

CHARACTERS

Narrator	Professor Collins
Hadley	Jordan
Lane	Chorus 1
Min	Chorus 2
Carmen	Chorus 3

Narrator: Several explorers, a professor, and a photographer from a nature Web site are standing at the mouth of a dark cave.

Professor Collins: Welcome, explorers, to the amazing world of speleology (SPEE•lee•AH•luh•jee), or the study of caves. This is Min, a video photographer from a well-known nature Web site. She'll be filming our explorations today.

Hadley: I think your Web site's walk-through exhibit of a cave is an incredible achievement.

Min: Why, thank you, but this is actually my first trip into a cave! ❶

Stop and Think

❶ What opinion does Hadley share?

Hadley shares the opinion that _____

_____

_____

Jordan: Do you know that cave explorers are called *spelunkers*?

Narrator: The spelunkers enter the dark cavern.

Chorus 1: Follow me, Min.

Chorus 2: No, this is the proper direction.

Chorus 3: Wait, I've found a better route.

Hadley: Wait, explorers! Stop bickering.

Professor Collins: Wherever we explore will be interesting, but let's start with the main path.

Chorus 1: All right then, Professor, lead on. ❷

Stop and Think

❷ What happens when the explorers enter the cave?

The explorers _____

_____

_____

Narrator: With Professor Collins in the lead, the explorers proceed down the dark tunnel.

Professor Collins: Watch your heads now. Bumping into a stalactite can leave a really nasty gash.

Min: Could someone please explain to me what a stalactite is? I'm afraid my understanding of caves is insufficient.

Carmen: A stalactite is like a stone icicle hanging from the roof of the cave.

Jordan: It can take thousands of years for a large stalactite to form. Mineral-rich water drips down and slowly hardens into this slender stone formation. **3**

Stop and Think

3 How are stalactites formed? Use your own words.

Stalactites are formed when _____

_____

_____

Hadley: Stalactites can be colored by the different minerals, too. They can be red, blue, yellow, or other hues.

Lane: Can stalactites also grow on the floor of a cave?

Carmen: No, those are called stalag*mites*. A stalagmite forms on the cave floor from falling water droplets.

Min: These stalagmites are so regal. That one looks like a throne for a king or queen.

Chorus 2: Film them so everyone can see them!

Narrator: The professor talks earnestly about responsible spelunking.

Professor Collins: We *must* not touch the fragile formations. **4**

Stop and Think

4 How are stalactites and stalagmites different?

Here is how they are different: _____

_____

_____

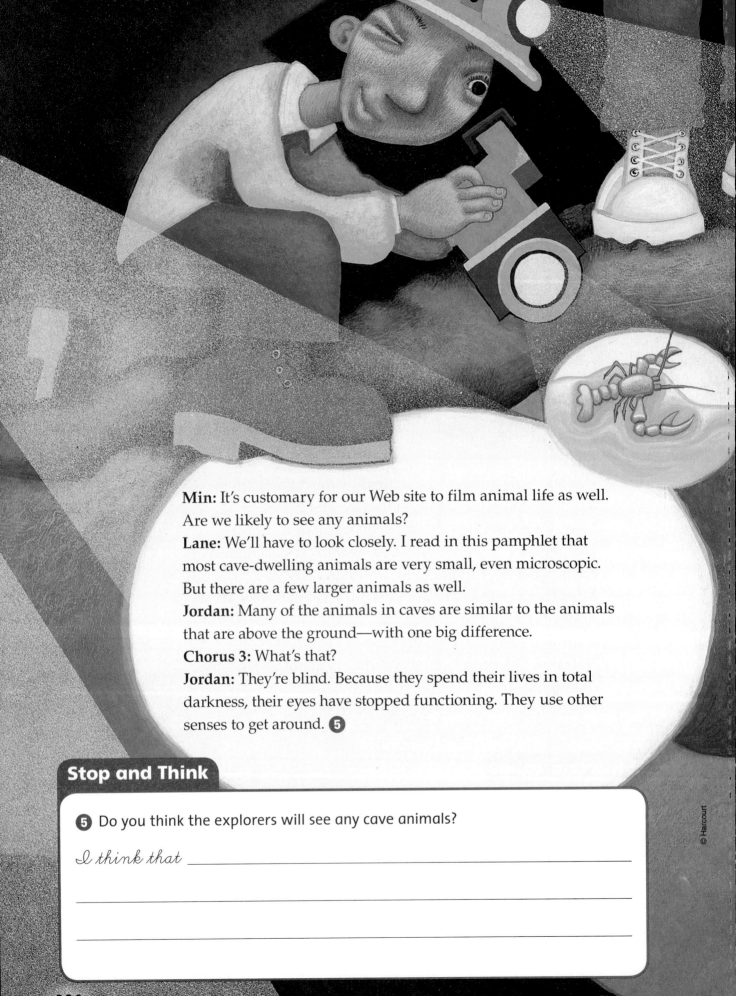

Min: It's customary for our Web site to film animal life as well. Are we likely to see any animals?

Lane: We'll have to look closely. I read in this pamphlet that most cave-dwelling animals are very small, even microscopic. But there are a few larger animals as well.

Jordan: Many of the animals in caves are similar to the animals that are above the ground—with one big difference.

Chorus 3: What's that?

Jordan: They're blind. Because they spend their lives in total darkness, their eyes have stopped functioning. They use other senses to get around. **5**

Stop and Think

5 Do you think the explorers will see any cave animals?

I think that _____

_____

_____

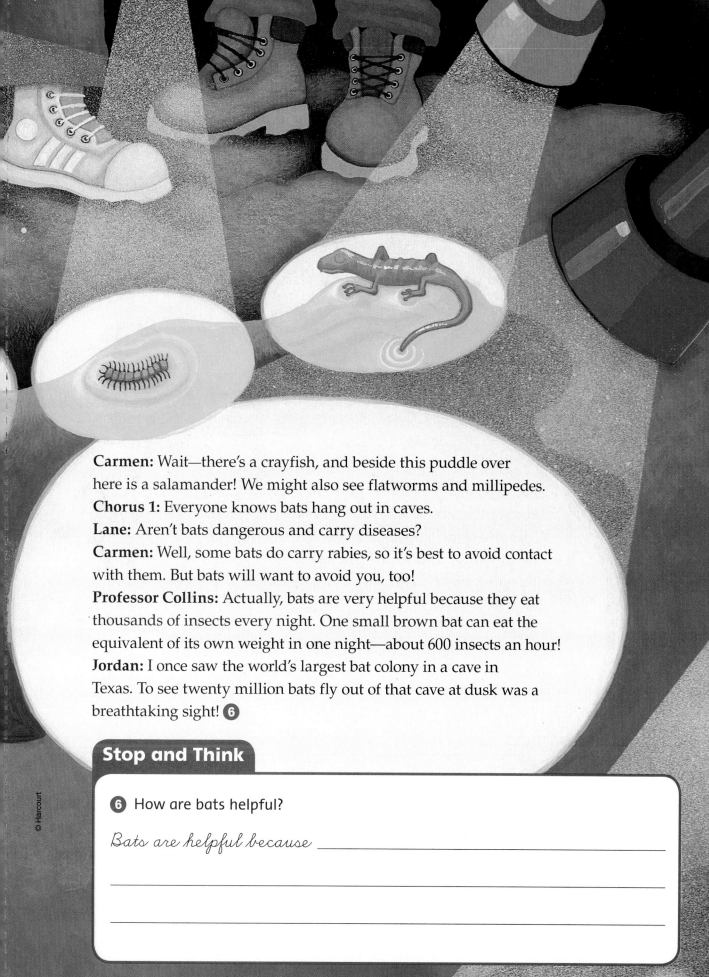

Carmen: Wait—there's a crayfish, and beside this puddle over here is a salamander! We might also see flatworms and millipedes.

Chorus 1: Everyone knows bats hang out in caves.

Lane: Aren't bats dangerous and carry diseases?

Carmen: Well, some bats do carry rabies, so it's best to avoid contact with them. But bats will want to avoid you, too!

Professor Collins: Actually, bats are very helpful because they eat thousands of insects every night. One small brown bat can eat the equivalent of its own weight in one night—about 600 insects an hour!

Jordan: I once saw the world's largest bat colony in a cave in Texas. To see twenty million bats fly out of that cave at dusk was a breathtaking sight! **6**

Stop and Think

6 How are bats helpful?

Bats are helpful because _____

_____

_____

Chorus 2: Shine your flashlights upwards, quickly!

Lane: What are all those furry bunches hanging upside down?

Hadley: Ummm, I believe they're Mexican free-tailed bats.

Min: Fantastic! Look how many of them there are! I've got to capture this exceptional sight on film!

Narrator: As Min excitedly films, the bats begin to fidget uneasily.

Min: I certainly hope we didn't provoke them. Is it customary for them to move around so much?

Hadley: Only when they're poised for flight.

Professor Collins: And I'd say they're getting ready now. . . .

Chorus 3: Duck, everybody, and make way for the bats! **7**

Stop and Think

7 What happens at the end of the selection?

At the end of the selection, _____

_____

_____

© Harcourt

308

Think Critically

1. What facts do the explorers learn about caves? MAIN IDEA
AND DETAILS

The explorers learn that _____

_____

_____

2. How are cave animals different from other animals? COMPARE
AND CONTRAST

Cave animals are different because _____

_____

_____

_____

3. How does this selection make you feel about exploring caves?
AUTHOR'S PURPOSE

It makes me feel _____

_____

_____

Photo Credits

Lesson 2

20 (br) doug steley/Alamy; 20 (l) Doug Steley/Alamy; 20 Duomo/CORBIS; 20 (r) Duomo/Corbis; 20 (l) Photodisc/Getty Images; 20 (c) Photodisc/Getty Images; 22 Newspix; 23 Newspix; 24 Newspix; 25 Newspix; 26 (t) Ian Waldie/REUTERS/Corbis; 27 Eric Gaillard/REUTERS/Corbis; 29 (tr) MERVYN REES/Alamy

Lesson 9

91 (b) Eleanor Caputo; 92 Anthony Dunn/Alamy; 93 (inset) Eleanor Caputo; 96 (l) California State Legislature; 96 (r) California State Legislature; 97 Spencer Grant/PhotoEdit

Lesson 12

122 Greg Probst/Corbis; 124 (cl) Animals Animals Earth Scenes; 124 (b) INSADCO Photography/Alamy; 124 (cr) W. Perry Conway/Corbis; 125 (t) Brandon D. Cole/Corbis; 125 (b) Divid Tipling/Alamy; 125 (b) Serge Vero/Alamy; 126 (t) Alaska Stock LLC/Alamy

Lesson 14

140 Konrad Wothe/Minden Pictures; 141 (br) Erich Schrempp/Photo Researchers, Inc.; 141 (c) foodfolio/Alamy; 141 (bl) Royalty-Free/Corbis; 142 (bg) KONRAD WOTHE/Minden Pictures; 143 (cr) Erich Schrempp/Photo Researchers, Inc.; 143 (cl) foodfolio/Alamy; 144 (bg) Panoramic Images/Getty Images; 144 (cr) Royalty Free/Corbis; 145 (cl) J Marshall-Tribaleye Images/Alamy; 145 (bl) John-Francis Bourke/zefa/Corbis; 145 (cr) Owaki-Kulla/CORBIS; 146 (cr) Envision/Corbis; 146 (bg) Momatiuk-Eastcott/Corbis; 146 (tr) Royalty-Free/Corbis; 148 (bg) Royalty-Free/Corbis; 148 (c) Royalty-Free/Corbis

Lesson 19

190 Courtesy of National Inventors Hall of Fame; 191 (b) Eastman Chemical Company; 192 SuperStock, Inc./SuperStock; 193 PhotoSpin, Inc./Alamy; 194 Courtesy of National Inventors Hall of Fame; 195 Hulton-Deutsch Collection/Corbis; 197 Eastman Chemical Company; 198 David Grace

Lesson 27

270 (r) Robert E. Peary Family Collection: Photographs Relating to the Nicaragua Canal Surveys, 1884–1888; National Archives Gift Collection of Materials relating to Polar Regions, 1949–1976; Record Group 401; National Archives; 271 (r) Robert Peary/National Geographic Image Collection; 272 (tr) Bettmann/Corbis; 272 (bg) Photo by Gordon Wiltsie/National Geographic/Getty Images; 273 (cl) Bettmann/Corbis; 273 (cr) Bettmann/Corbis; 274 (bg) Jerry Kobalenko/Getty Images; 274 (c) Robert Peary/National Geographic Image Collection; 275 (c) Robert Peary/National Geographic Image Collection; 276 (bg) Jerry Kobalenko/Getty images; 277 (t) Robert Peary/National Geographic Image Collection; 278 (bg) Alan Kearney/Getty Images; 278 (c) Robert E. Peary Family Collection: Photographs Relating to the Nicaragua Canal Surveys, 1884–1888; National Archives Gift Collection of Materials Relating to Polar Regions, 1949–1976 Record Group 401

Lesson 29

National Archives; 291 The Granger Collection, New York; 292 (bg) The Granger Collection, New York; 295 (c) Johnathan Drake/epa/Corbis; 296 (c) The Granger Collection, New York; 298 (bg) Historical Picture Archive/Corbis; 298 (br) Historical Picture Archive/Corbis; 298 (tr) Hulton Archive/Getty Images; 298 (cl) The Granger Collection, New York